Groupware

Business success with computer supported cooperative working

Joseph St John Bate and Nathan Travell

ALFRED WALLER LIMITED
HENLEY ON THAMES

Published by
Alfred Waller Limited
Orchards, Fawley, Henley on Thames
Oxfordshire RG9 6JF, Great Britain

First published 1994

ISBN 1 872474 12 8

British Library Cataloguing in Publication Data
A catalogue entry for this title is available from the British Library

Printed and bound in Great Britain by the Lavenham Press, Suffolk

To Pete, Teresa, Jo and Helen

Acknowledgements

We would like to take the opportunity to acknowledge the many people who have provided valuable input in the production of this book. We will name some here but we offer our appreciation to all our colleagues at PA Consulting Group and to all the authors whose books, papers and articles stimulated us into writing this publication and helped enormously during its production. We would most especially like to thank Garth Shephard for all his help, cooperation and understanding and explanation of the groupware infrastructure, Ross Burgess for the research work that he and Joe Bate did together in the 80s, AT&T, Donna Garten and Malcolm White without whose help and availability this could not have been possible, John Kay, Mark Roberts and Geoff Vincent of PA Consulting Group for their excellent input, members of Regus Computer Services for positively proof reading the document and the many groupware software and hardware vendors whose products and innovation spurred us into writing.

Preface

The introduction of groupware products is being hailed as the start of a new beginning. The ability to allow employees to work effectively as a team and to allow the sharing of information across the breadth of the organisation is seen as a significant step in achieving better customer service and increased productivity in addition to other remarkable benefits.

The groupware market place is currently expanding at a phenomenal rate and it appears as though this is set to continue. Market researchers IDC estimate that the market will be worth $600m in the US in 1995 compared with just $11m in 1991. Groupware consultants Workgroup Technologies put the figure even higher at $2bn in 1995.

This explosion has caused widespread confusion among senior managers and many Information Technology (IT) professionals alike. Suppliers are all claiming that their products provide the perfect groupware solution, consultants are selling their services in the areas of cultural change and business process reengineering but there are only a small number of people who actually understand the concepts of groupware and how to realise the broad range of benefits that it can bring.

This book aims to remedy the situation by providing a clear definition of groupware, outlining the technology categories which make up the groupware market place and giving detailed procedures that can be followed to achieve a successful groupware implementation. It focuses on the assessment of organisational structure and culture and how this needs to be transformed in order to maximise the benefits obtained from groupware. Its intentions are to :

- explain why the introduction of groupware products into an organisation is of fundamental importance

- assess the structural and cultural organisational changes that are involved with a groupware implementation
- demonstrate the best mechanisms for the assessment of a work group's characteristics
- outline the necessary steps in achieving a successful groupware pilot
- provide a framework, in the form of the Groupware Pyramid Principle, which can be used to implement a groupware solution successfully.

The book is primarily aimed at senior managers and IT professionals involved in the first stages of a groupware implementation, i.e., considering the benefits that can be achieved or analysing the impact that the implementation will have on the organisation's structure and culture, but it will also appeal to a much wider audience. Specifically, those individuals who:

- have an interest in groupware and want to know more
- are already involved in an existing groupware project
- want to increase their general knowledge of the IT industry and the recent developments in it.

A brief history of groupware

Although only recently gaining mass recognition in the market place, the origins of groupware can be traced back to the 1960s when pioneering work was being carried out in the area of Computer Supported Cooperative Work (CSCW). Among others, Douglas Englebart, (the originator of the 'mouse' pointer and widely recognised as the father of the groupware concept), and his team at the Stanford Research Institute carried out a number of projects centred around the On-Line System (NLS). NLS was designed to support a team of people drawn from different disciplines by providing them with a core set of software tools such as a text editor, graphics program and data managers. The research on NLS influenced further work at Xerox's Palo Alto Research Centre which eventually led to the development of the Apple Macintosh and Microsoft Windows.

Englebart's original aim was to 'augment individuals doing knowledge work'. As networking became available, NLS was extended to support groups of knowledge workers who could communicate via the network, arguably making it the first form of Groupware. NLS let researchers work together on a project and develop ideas by cooperating with each other through the system.

Since this early work, groupware can be seen to have evolved along with the advances in hardware technology which have made enhanced forms of communication and collaboration possible.

In the 1960s, data processing systems were introduced on traditional mainframe platforms. These applications were typically based on large navigational databases, transaction processing and access from character-based terminals. This type of system - now known as legacy systems - ruled corporate IT for many years and in many large businesses remains a prominent part of their IT infrastructure and future plans.

Word processing made its appearance in the late 1970s and became an established software tool in most offices during the 1980s. It had a dramatic effect on the productivity of administration staff who suddenly had the capability to store and subsequently amend documents, maintain a collection of frequently used documents and use mail merge facilities to distribute them. Word processing in its various forms along with spreadsheet and personal database facilities now forms the foundation of most office-based IT.

'Traditional' office automation (OA) products arrived during the 1980s with systems such as Data General Corp.'s CEO Office, Digital Equipment Corp.'s All-In-1, IBM's PROFS and Wang Laboratories Inc.'s Office all combining word processing with shared filing and electronic mail capabilities. Some would argue that these represent the first commercially available forms of groupware but we hope to demonstrate that groupware has a lot more to offer than the traditional OA systems.

Perhaps the biggest revolution in office based computing occurred in the early 1980s with the introduction of the personal computer. This brought personal computing to the masses and gave office workers the ability to increase their productivity by providing them with feature rich, user friendly software tools. By the end of this decade PCs had become established as major business tools and had rooted themselves firmly in the offices of most companies.

The Explosion of Technologies

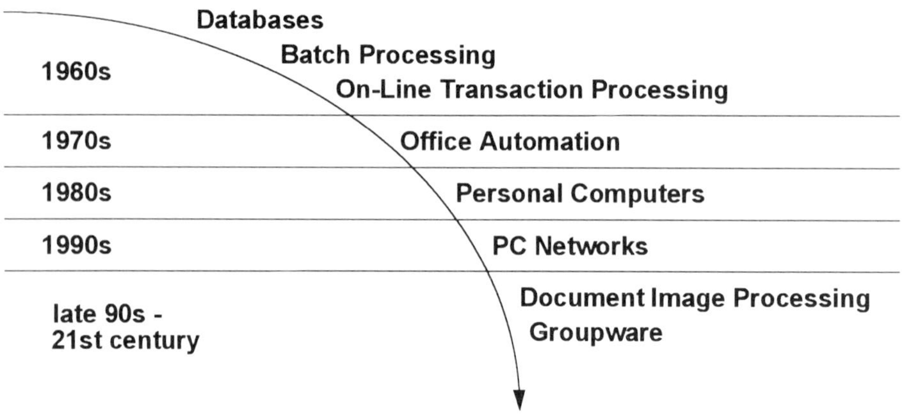

The next significant stage in the evolution of office based IT involved the introduction of networking. Since the latter part of the 1980s and the early 1990s more and more PCs have been networked in some way, providing users with facilities such as shared filing and electronic mail. The number of PCs currently being networked is growing at a staggering rate and recent surveys have concluded that by 1996, up to 90 per cent of all PCs could be connected to some form of network.

Most organisations have gone through these different generations of IT with the result being a hotch potch of systems addressing different parts of a single problem in an unconnected way. Even some of the more recent technologies that have appeared such as document image processing, workflow management and text retrieval have not helped in this problem. Instead, they have simply served to add yet another isolated and uncoordinated system designed around improving certain types of tasks.

Groupware is positioned to become the technology of the late 1990s. The expansion in networked PCs, advancements in communication facilities and the realisation that team working is the way to achieve business success will provide the basis upon which it will grow. Many market research companies predict that groupware will comprise the largest IT market place at the beginning of the next century and many prominent figures have commented that:

> "Companies which have not yet begun to consider the 'groupware environment' or 'groupware solution' should start soon or be left behind".

Why the groupware explosion?

We have just said that the origins of groupware can be traced back over 30 years - so why has it only recently begun to take off? There a number of reasons for this apparently sudden recognition:

- the division between the demand for groupware products and the availability of the technology required to implement them has become progressively smaller
- the technological infrastructure necessary for groupware to succeed has matured and become readily available at affordable prices
- organisations have begun to realise that their structure and culture must change to meet the business demands of the 90s
- many companies are moving to client-server architectures and opting for open systems platforms - the architecture which is ideal for groupware
- the importance of corporate information and the need to share it has become more apparent - information is useless until it is shared
- it is now recognised that 'empowered' teams of individuals working collectively to achieve common business objectives are significantly more productive than employees working in isolation - groupware provides the framework for individuals to work effectively as a team.

Outline of the book

The main emphasis of the book is on providing the reader with the framework and knowledge needed to successfully implement a groupware solution from the stage of considering the benefits that the technology can bring, to widespread implementation throughout an organisation. In providing this framework, we concentrate on assessing the culture and structure of an organisation and managing the subsequent change in it to prepare for a groupware implementation. We believe that this is the most important and crucial stage of a groupware implementation and that without the correct culture and structure in place, groupware is likely to 'fail'. We are concerned with giving the reader sufficient understanding to facilitate the successful implementation of a groupware solution and the contents and structure of the book are driven towards this aim.

We have devised a basic groupware methodology, the Groupware Pyramid Principle, which can be used as the framework for a successful groupware implementation. The methodology consists of four stages which should be completed in order to realise the full potential of a groupware solution. Three of the stages provide a foundation upon which the fourth stage, company wide implementation, can be built. The book is structured around this principle, with sections III to VI reflecting each of the four building blocks needed to reach the 'groupware pinnacle'.

The book begins in Section I by presenting a description of the traditional office structure that is still prominent in many organisations and highlighting the deficiencies of this. The analysis concentrates on the psychology of the white collar worker and their desire to compete, to be the best and thus withhold from their peers information that could impede this goal. The ways in which groupware eliminates the problems of the traditional office and helps an organisation move from 'isolation individualism' to 'collaborative individualism' are then considered.

Section II introduces groupware to the reader: its definition, the reasons for its dramatic appearance in the market place, the tasks that it helps to perform and the technologies that comprise the groupware market place. The Groupware Pyramid Principle is also introduced in this section along with details of how this can be exploited to achieve a successful groupware implementation.

To achieve success from groupware, it is essential that prior to the implementation, a groupware environment is adopted. This is the area that Section III concentrates on; how to create the right environment for the introduction of groupware. Moving to a groupware environment involves analysing the current organisational structure and culture and adapting this to suit the groupware concept. We believe that a fundamental element in this process is the analyses of the individual work groups and their particular characteristics so that the appropriate groupware technologies can be selected. We give a technique for performing these analyses and detail how particular groupware technologies can be mapped to the identified characteristics.

Establishing the ideal environment for groupware to be successful is probably the most difficult but also the most important stage in a groupware project. Once this hurdle has been overcome, implementation can begin; this is no easy task in itself though. Selecting a pilot system is essential to this part of the process as is managing the change that will occur and implementing the necessary education programmes throughout the organisation. For groupware to be adopted across the breadth of the company, it is imperative that the pilot system is a great success. Section IV deals with the issues surrounding this area.

Most organisations do not have the IT architecture and infrastructure necessary to remain competitive and take their business successfully into the next century. Without a reliable, efficient, robust and scaleable infrastructure, businesses will not be able to respond to the increasingly volatile market places that will begin to dominate the end of this decade. Many companies do not appreciate this fact and have jumped on the groupware bandwagon, implementing applications before an adequate infrastructure has been established. This has resulted in insignificant productivity gains and an even more disparate and isolated IT architecture. In Section V, we present the types of IT architecture which need to be in place to realise the full potential of groupware and lead an organisation into the 21st century.

The marketing hype surrounding groupware would lead one to believe that a groupware solution will reap rewards regardless of when, how and why it was implemented. This is not necessarily the case. Justifying a groupware implementation and measuring the resulting benefits can be difficult as many of the advantages are intangible but still provide significant gains in business performance, employee satisfaction and client service. Benefits have to be identified and quantified to justify the expenditure and also to promote the expansion of groupware into other parts of the organisation. In Section VI we present some justification techniques that take into account the nature of groupware benefits and also identify a number of the advantages that groupware can bring. We also highlight the techniques by which the benefits can be adequately measured and reported, and document some of those experienced by organisations which have already implemented a groupware solution.

New developments in the IT industry are always introduced along with claims of increased productivity, better customer service and many other such statements, but few if any have lived up to these claims. Will groupware be different? Will groupware help deliver the increased worker productivity which has been realised in the manufacturing industry but has yet to result from significant investments in IT? Will groupware create corporate structures and cultures capable of meeting the business demands of the next century?

With the vast sums of money currently being poured into the groupware market by suppliers, consultancies and clients, it is guaranteed not to be a short term solution. Whether it will succeed in answering the above questions has yet to be determined - the technology is still relatively new. In Section VII we conclude the discussions in this book and look to the future in an attempt to predict the impact that groupware will have and the 21st century office that it will create.

Table of contents

Section I. Is the 20th Century White Collar Worker Doomed?

Chapter 1. The white collar worker dominates the 20th century

The business structure of the 20th century has been built around the office and the office worker.

The business office now dominates our lives. Our cities are commanded by towering concrete and glass office blocks, overshadowing the churches and cathedrals that once dominated our environment and lives. The skylines of our cities are recognised by the silhouettes of these offices that, like giant teeth, penetrate all aspects of our lives. These silhouettes are the icons of the 20th century. But will this be the case in the 21st century?

At the beginning of the this century, offices as we know them barely existed, and few people worked in them. Today they run everything, or, at the very least, are at the heart of everything that is run. Offices are without doubt, one of the strongest forces that shape the civilised world today. The many and varied office organisations - financial, commercial, government, business and municipal - impinge upon almost every facet of our daily routines. Approximately half of the UK work force works in or from an office. But will this be the case during the 21st century?

Today, everyone is affected in some way or other by an office organisation and its administrative procedures. Details of name, address, date of birth, credit rating, medical history, driving licence, criminal record or whatever are held on numerous paper files in offices by both government and private business. Indeed offices, or rather the information contained in those offices, are vital to every citizen. Offices are the nub of our civilisation. And the white collar worker is the priest of business information management.

1.1 White collar workers manage information

The white collar worker manages information and uses it to enable society. This information can be used for a variety of purposes, many of which allows a citizen to function in society. Your health, credit rating, social security entitlement, education, employment prospects, goods and services are all affected by the information contained in these offices and the way in which the information is applied.

We may question the right of organisations to hold records of information about us, without our knowing exactly what they contain; indeed there is a strong movement in many countries to place limits on the way in which personal information is held and used. However most of us would be very upset if some vital piece of information were not available when required. This could be a medical record in the event of being suddenly admitted to hospital, or details about pension or insurance policies when our financial situation required them most.

Information contained in offices is not only vital to individuals but is also a crucial part of any organisation. An organisation needs information just as an engine needs petrol - or, as the 21st century arrives, did need petrol. If you examine the many vast military organisations throughout the world, you find that their main task is to gather, analyse and process data. The ratio of ten office workers to each soldier in the field is a reflection of the size of the task. When the military organisation of Eastern Europe collapsed, the problem was not what to do with the military personnel, since they had many engineering and practical skills, but how to absorb the vast numbers of white collar support workers - 'office workers'.

1.2 Offices today are under threat

Despite being so important, both to organisations and to members of society, offices are currently under threat - or is it the office workers who should be worried? They are horrendously expensive, and their productivity is low and stagnant. Senior management regularly examines very carefully all aspects of their businesses, and now, increasingly they are scrutinising the office and the way in which it functions.

A close examination of the office reveals a number of points that are increasingly becoming the concern of top management, and this is an implied threat to everyone who works in an office. One of these is that administrative costs are increasing at the rate of 10 to 15 per cent per annum. And of the total administrative costs, nearly 60 per cent are attributable to managerial and professional salaries, and the fringe benefits that go with them. The question top management, fund managers and shareholders are increasingly asking, is 'What are we getting for our money? How can we improve our return?'

The question leads to a disturbing answer: the current increase in productivity in the office is so meagre, even after a decade of office automation, that it cannot match the increased demands placed on offices - let alone the salary increases demanded by office workers. Already the white collar labour force is approximately 45 per cent of the total labour force, and up until the late eighties was still growing. That is not the case now. The question all office workers must ask is will the office survive in the 21st century or will they be abandoned by society like the churches of previous centuries, as organisations develop new ways of processing information.

1.2.1 Professional white collar workers at risk

After more than a decade of ruthlessly cutting blue collar workers, senior executives discovered that the logical slimming head count does not stop on the shop floor. Throughout the world there is a drive to reduce cost and that increasingly means reducing the white collar workers' head count. This is borne out by bleak news for the managerial classes as one announcement after another is made that layers of management are being reduced with many staff being made redundant. The axe will fall most heavily on departmental managers and their staff who deal with paper shuffling activities.

'We want more people dealing with the customer and fewer people filling in pieces of paper' is a quote that has been heard more than once.

What is new is the scale of the change. It has accelerated because of the extreme pressure on costs and the rate that technology has been advancing. Many of the most successful IT implementations have provided an automated and integrated process from start through to finish, i.e., recording sales through ordering and storing to manufacture. The need for paper in duplicate and triplicate and the many offices where these pieces of paper were processed, has disappeared - so have the white collar workers, including their senior bosses.

The scale with which companies have been unloading their most senior people has prompted some analysts and commentators to suspect that the profession of management is now redundant. There are those who think that the whole middle management might well disappear since the approach to the restructuring of large multi-national corporations is to strip out layers of middle management. The trend is not just restricted to Britain, Europe and America, the Japanese are also suffering the first of a wave of redundancies.

1.3 Globalisation means competition

Companies have automated the blue collar workers and reduced staff, they have changed the ways in which they work and now there is no more leeway on that front. As competition becomes more global and more intense they are having to move on to middle managers and senior managers to cut costs. This means automating and changing the way in which they work. Groupware can be central to this process.

When it comes to staff cuts, the British telecommunications company BT is perhaps the most dramatic example. The company was privatised in 1984 when it employed a total of 244,000 people. In 1994 it has 153,000 workers with the bulk of the cuts falling on operators, clerical staff and engineers. Slowly the company has been moving up the hierarchy. In the past two years 5,000 middle managers and 1,000 senior managers have been removed. This process has not stopped. Just because managers have nice jobs, are well paid and are not worried about finding alternative employment, it will not stop them being the targets of cost reduction exercises. The role and job content of senior staff in organisations are changing. Instead of managing to survive, people will become professionals who can deliver measurable benefit to the organisation. To support this work pattern they will need new types of IT which can support the new ways of working. Groupware can be central to this process.

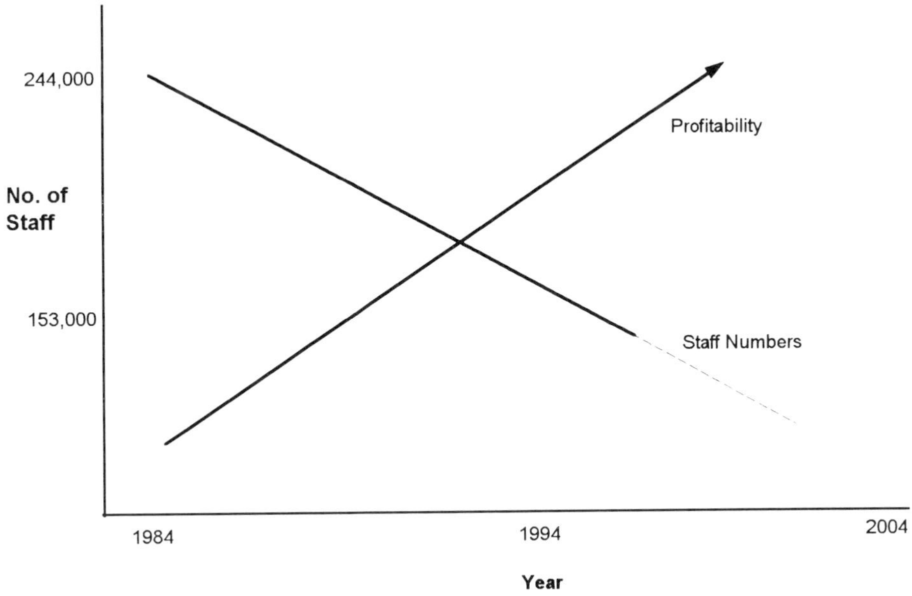

Figure 1.1 Staff cuts at BT - a model for the future?

1.3.1 Competition means the need for more accurate information

Against this background, all organisations are demanding steadily more information each year about markets, customers, products, competitors and much more. A measure of the magnitude of this demand is that, every year, more than 200 billion telephone calls are made, over 140 billion documents are created, in excess of two million new scientific facts are discovered and thousands of new products are put on to the market. These figures are not only staggering in themselves, but are increasing every year and show no sign of stopping.

Within a paper based environment all the information being generated has to be stored in some filing cabinet or other; often not once but many times. One reason for this is that many people and groups of people feel that they will require some of the information, but they do not know exactly which information. The 80/20 rule tends to apply in this situation. That is, 80 per cent of the need will be met by only 20 per cent of the information - the problem is to decide which 20 per cent.

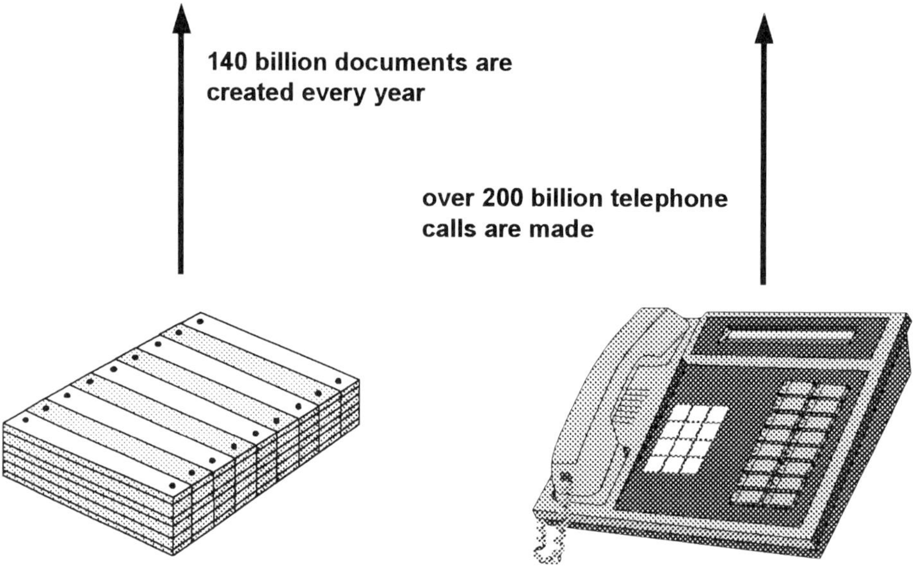

Figure 1.2 Information is continually increasing

All this information is not just stored; it has to be handled in the various offices throughout the world by office workers. We use the word 'handled' advisedly since it is in most cases a manual task. The physical work expended, making and receiving these telephone calls; creating, editing and distributing the billions of paper documents; classifying and filing the millions of facts, to mention a few of the office tasks, is immense. It is this labour-intensive nature of the office that makes it particularly sensitive to escalating costs. However an important point in history has been reached: recent technological developments offer for the first time a number of dramatic opportunities to avoid or at least to reduce these escalating costs; to provide information more quickly and more accurately. Groupware could be one of these breakthroughs.

To control costs, and to provide information quickly and accurately, is increasingly becoming the main goals for the management of any organisation. These goals are now within reach, by the sensible application of IT which in many cases will include groupware.

1.4 Changes in organisational structures and support technologies

All useful technologies have to support the organisational structure and since the organisational structure in offices is changing, so also are the support technologies. Groupware will be one of the support technologies. But what is groupware? Does it exist?

Groupware is still developing and changing because the management structure it will have to support is still developing and changing. But groupware does exist and it is developing. It has the potential to be a major force in changing the way in which the functions of the office are undertaken.

There is a need for all white collar workers to understand the potential of groupware and how it could be used in their work environment to increase the efficiency of themselves and of their organisation. The alternative will be to use their energies to identify other employment opportunities.

This book sets out to help them in that quest by explaining the importance and opportunities of groupware, how it can help them to increase their personal productivity by working in cooperation with their peers, how team working will begin to dominate the office organisation and the ways in which groupware may change their working lives.

Chapter 2. New processes required for 21st century

2.1 The increasing complexity of business requirements

Business life today is more complex than ever before. International trade is becoming more important, exchange rates and prices fluctuate more wildly, the time to market is reducing and there are ever-increasing government or international regulations to be adhered to. The framework for business decision-making is more complex than ever. And increasingly, decisions must be made, and information communicated, extremely quickly.

The progress of technology itself has increased the pressure. Advanced technologies reduce the boundaries between national markets and alter customer expectations. They now have and demand more choice. Not long ago, for example, life insurance companies offered basically two products, term and whole life. Today, they supply a vast number of specialist products to fit market niches or the needs of small clearly defined groups of customers. Although globalisation is one trend another is the fragmentation of the market into niche groups who expect and demand products to suit their exact requirements and life style. This trend also creates competitive pressures on organisations. These competitive pressures are increasingly forcing insurance companies, along with everyone else, to create new products.

Is groupware just a new product looking for a market or does it attempt to fill a real requirement?

The pace of change continues to accelerate with the globalisation of the economy; all companies face greater numbers of competitors, each one of which is attempting to deliver innovative products and services to the market place. Product cycles have gone from years to months and customers that used to accept products and services that were an appropriate fit, now demand a much closer fit, to satisfy their every changing requirements In this environment good performers will drive out poor performers.

The point is that not only have the life cycles of products and services reduced, but so has the time to develop and introduce new products and services; the emphasis now is on speed to market.

2.2 The flow of information has to be managed

In the fast-moving world of today, reliance on traditional paper-based communications and decision making processes, traditional organisational and decision making structures are just no longer good enough. In the nineteenth century, when the race was on to get the first tea samples to the London tea market, success went to the firm who had invested in the best sailing-ship technology for its tea clippers. In the 21st century, information transfer will be the key factor, and success will increasingly depend on using fast and efficient techniques for the processing and movement of all forms of information.

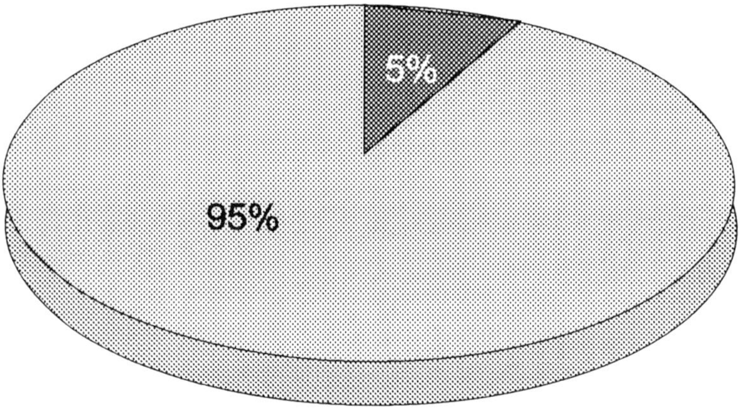

Figure 2.1 Only 5 per cent of information is held electronically

Yet, to date, automation has not proceeded very fast in the office. If we compare the investment per worker in different sectors, we find that the value of capital equipment per office worker is one twelfth the value per factory worker, and one thirtieth the value per farm worker.

What is more, such investment as has happened in office automation, has been unevenly distributed. There have been computer systems to assist (or replace) the work of clerks and there have been word processing systems to assist secretaries and typists. There have been many personal computers to assist the managers and executives, whose time is far more expensive, and who have far greater scope for affecting the future of the organisation by the quality of the decisions they make and the information they use to arrive at those decisions. However, in the majority of cases these personal computers have remained personal and have not been integrated into a system that could increase productivity. What is required is a new way of doing business or reengineering the business. Groupware could be the a way in which this is achieved. It is not just the case that groupware provides an opportunity to reengineer the business but that this is a prerequisite to applying groupware successfully; otherwise groupware will deliver no more than the traditional office systems.

2.3 Business reengineering comes to life with communications

Many studies have found that managers spend a very large part of their time communicating - perhaps up to 80 per cent. A more surprising statistic, perhaps, is that up to 90 per cent of this communication is with members of their own organisation. Consequently, if groupware and its associated IT infrastructure is to have a substantial effect to enable managers and executives to become more effective, it will need to concentrate particularly on communications, and communications within the organisation should be the initial focus of attention.

2.3.1 Will there be office desks in the future?

Will there be an office desk in the workgroup enabled offices of the near future? We believe that, contrary to predictions by futurologists, sociologists and the like, there will be desks in the office for a long time to come. However, there is increasing evidence that the desks will be completely different to those of today and that the term 'office' will have a different meaning and image than at present.

The offices and the furniture used during the 20th century were designed to accommodate the flow of information on paper.

Groupware will part of the office environment that manages the flow of information electronically. The office and the furniture in a groupware enabled environment will be different - very different.

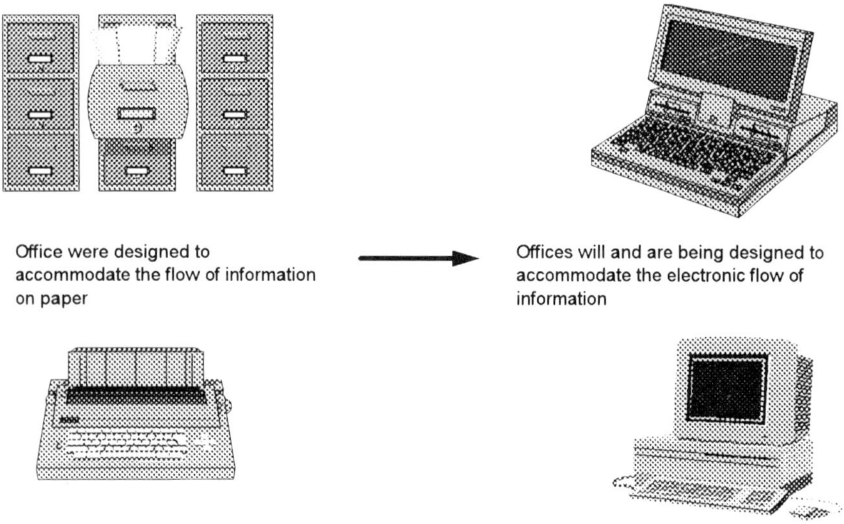

Figure 2.2 The 'New Office' will be designed for electronic information flows

2.3.2 The days when the office meant paper

In the days when the office meant paper, and in truth this still means almost any office today, the many different types of office activity were physically separated. The secretary with her PC and word processing package (instead of a typewriter) dealing with correspondence and text generation. The accountant with his spreadsheet (instead of calculator) and ability to manipulate figures. The storeman with his stock control terminal(s) (instead of many inventory lists). The executive with his communications to headquarters and instructions to the operators in the field. Although physically separate they were bound together by the use of a common medium to communicate information.

Traditionally this has been paper, although it is slowly changing. The paper based communication packages may not have been a standard shape, size, layout or colour but it is a common medium with a standard 'operating system' for displaying information, namely the written (or typed) word. This means that the written word or message, and therefore the information that each office worker produces and uses, can be recognised and processed. The inefficiencies and inflexibilities of the paper process is caused by the paper - what is needed is a new medium and a new super highway to transport the medium.

2.4 Information flows

Various studies have found that communication of one sort or another is by far the most important single element of white collar work. To go back to fundamentals, the essence of communication is to present information to another person in such a way that they can understand it and at a time and place where the information is required. And that, as most people find out, is far from an easy task. This is one of the reasons why people congregate in the office. One of the goals of groupware is to provide a mechanism to display information in a way that is understood and is available where and when it is required in order that it may be processed and the resulting decision made available instantaneously.

2.4.1 Decoupling gives flexibility

Many of the most important advances in office technology, of which groupware is one, have had the effect of 'decoupling' the person communicating from the person receiving the information, in respect of space, time or both. This separation brings with it a new set of problems and a new set of opportunities: both need to be understood.

> "advances in office automation have had the effect of 'decoupling' the person communicating from the person receiving in respect of space, time or both" [*Bate and Burgess 1985*]

With ordinary or unaided speech, both parties have to be present at the same place and time. This immediacy of communication was first broken with the invention of writing, which allowed speech to be recorded for a later time. This invention, the recording of information (which started as graphics but developed into writing) was probably the single most important invention in the history of the human race. This is because it enabled facts and knowledge and therefore information to be recorded and used at a latter date, independent of individuals' memory. This has allowed each new generation to build upon the existing knowledge accumulated by previous ages.

The growth of reliable postal services developed the capabilities of the written word, by permitting communication at a distance. Speeded up by the industrial revolution, it greatly helped in the development of trade. Even today vast amounts of business are carried out or greatly aided by the postal service. However, even in the early part of this century, postal delays had begun to hamper business. Today, as the speed of commercial life increases, the slowness of the postal service is becoming a serious problem.

2.4.2 Paper is too slow

Traditional paper-based communications are too slow for today's business needs. This is for two main reasons: firstly, if we are holding information on paper we need to physically transport the paper to where the information is needed, and this takes time, even with today's airmail and fax machines; secondly, the process of getting paper transported involves a great deal of handling, sorting, batching, and waiting, as well as the actual time it is in transit.

2.4.3 The medium is the message

Different types of medium have different styles associated with them. This is partly a matter of cost or lack of space, for example, the extreme brevity of newspaper headlines. There are also other factors; for example being separated in time from the recipient allows you more time for planning and careful choice of words in a letter, as compared to a telephone conversation.

Another way of looking at the office is to examine the various processes that take place, the ways in which they inter-relate, and the skills used by the various office staff to carry out these processes. In this way we can build up a picture of the way in which the office operates within an organisation.

Many traditional writers have described the office as a mixture of unrelated activities. But this misses the point that the office or the collection of offices are the information centres of every organisation that functions in a coherent fashion. However, they can become islands of information all too easily in which case they will not function in a coherent fashion. At present most offices mainly deal with paper-based information, even if they have to print it from the computer first. Office workers still think in terms of paper and paper processes.

Office workers receive, process, store, file, retrieve, and distribute this paper based information within a hierarchical management structure. The structure is based on tradition but also reflects the needs of paper based information system - it is inefficient, costly and slow and is therefore not suited to the needs of the 21st century.

2.5 People and pyramidal organisations

The standard pyramidal organisational structure of most organisations is mirrored in all of the organisations and departments within it. These are the roots of today's corporation and stem from the belief that the Adam Smith way to increase productivity is, if not the only way, certainly the best. This process of splitting work and providing layers of supervisory staff tends to thin slice work into meaningless units of activity. The purpose of these activities is lost and in an office environment, the measurements of success becomes distorted. This results in low productivity and inappropriate work activities.

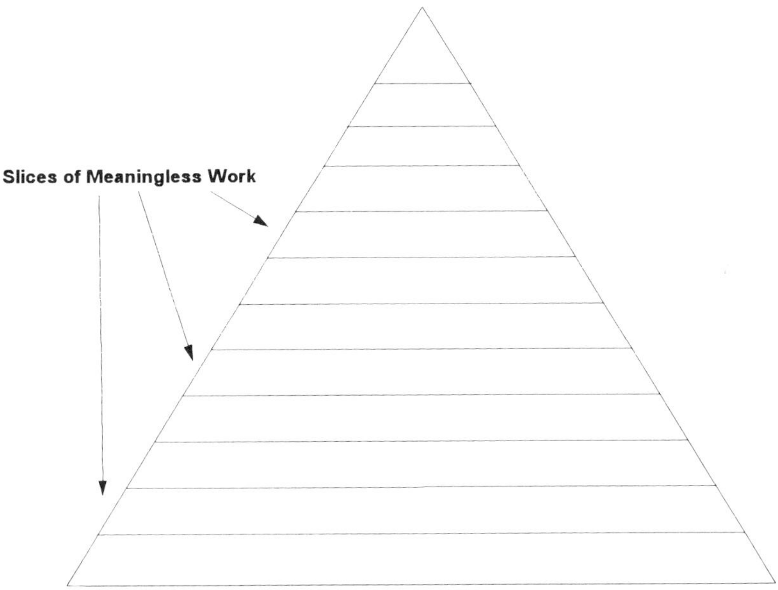

Figure 2.3 Slices of meaningless work

If modern companies thin slice work into meaningless tasks it was because this was how efficiency was once achieved. If they diffuse power and responsibility through massive bureaucracies, it is because that was the way they learnt to control sprawling enterprises. If they resist suggestions that they change the way they operate, it is because the organisational principles and structures have worked well for generations. But will they work in the future? The answer is no. A new paradigm will be required for all organisations who wish to remain competitive.

2.6 There has to be another answer

Many organisations and people think that automation is the answer to business problems. True, computers can speed up work, and in the past forty years, billions have been spent automating tasks that people once did by hand. Automation does get some jobs faster, but fundamentally the same jobs are being done, using the same processes and that means no fundamental improvements in performance.

2.6.1 Thin slicing work into meaningless tasks

To illustrate let us look at a task found in practically every company in the world - fulfilling an order. It begins when a customer places an order and ends when the goods and services are delivered and it includes everything that occurs in between. Typically the process involves a dozen or so steps performed by different people in different departments. The sales office receives the order, logs it in and checks it for completeness and accuracy. The order then undergoes a credit check and then the price of the order is calculated. It then has to travel to inventory control to find out if the product or service is available. If it isn't, the order gets routed to the production department which issues a back order. Eventually warehouse operations develops a shipping order. And transport determines the shipping method. Product handling picks the products from the warehouse, verifies the accuracy of the order, assembles the picking and loads them. Transport releases the goods to the carrier which undertakes to deliver them to the customer. The process maybe complex but when viewed from division of labour principles it does have certain advantages. It also has many disadvantages and although the tasks require automation, and in many cases these tasks have been computerised, benefits are slow to arrive.

What is required is the development of new ways of achieving the fundamental task - which is to process an order as quickly and inexpensively as possible in a way which will satisfy the customer and maximise the return for the organisation.. This will require business reengineering - and that is much more of a challenge. The task is to make these important activities more meaningful to those that have to carry them out and enable them to be more productive. To undertake to do the same tasks more effectively, with fewer people at a lower cost.

2.7 Creation as the starting point

The start point for changing or reengineering the business functions involves the creation of ideas, the thought process. But what has to be tackled is changing the way in which the business functions and then develop the office procedures to support these functions - even to the extent that the office will no longer exist. Groupware could be instrumental in that process. However, it is necessary to have a framework or understanding of the fundamental activities that occur.

2.7.1 Capture of information

The fundamental process is the capture of the information. This is a prelude to the information being communicated to some process desk. There is no point capturing information unless you are going to communicate it in some form or the other. The process of capturing information involves using some communication medium: usually paper, but it is increasingly done using a terminal or OCR reader or image capture. It could equally be by speaking on the telephone or at a meeting or conference. If it is captured on paper it will be captured many times. Even in this day and age of computerisation how many times have you given the same organisation your name and address?

These are all very different methods of capturing information, and each of them requires different skills and different capture mediums. Many people who are involved in these areas have not acquired the skills. Their performance suffers because of this, as does the performance of those to whom they wish to communicate. An immensely important point, that is often not fully understood, is that the material has to be prepared and presented in a way in which it can be understood by those who are to receive it. This involves presenting the material in an accurate and pleasing manner. There is nothing worse (unless you suffer from insomnia) than having to sit through an ill-prepared speech by an incompetent speaker. But in terms of the cost to business, in wasted time and missed opportunities, failures in the use of the written word are far more serious. In our own business of computers and new technology we have seen all too often the disastrous consequences of inadequate specifications and missing or out-of-date documentation.

The amount of paper swimming around our offices has been doubling every seven years, and this is during a time when so-called informed commentators were forecasting the advent of the paper-less office. The amount of paper in circulation is threatening to cause a thrombosis in the office. The photocopier has one benefit that outweighs all its disadvantages, which is that it helps in the dissemination of information throughout an organisation. However the photocopier and the word processing software packages have a great deal to answer for in the generation of paper. There must be a question mark in those organisations that do keep some semblance of control over photocopiers, as to whether the photocopier is an advantage or a disadvantage. Like so many other things in this world it is a double-edged sword, it helps in distributing information but it also clutters up filing cabinets and clogs the communication arteries. Unstructured e-mail does not help and is an example of automating a process and getting little benefit, when instead of reengineering the process using existing technology.

2.8 Search and retrieval

The way information is stored in paper-based files and many non-relational databases makes information retrieval a highly complex and difficult task. Filing is vital, since information retrieval depends on the accuracy and logic of the way it is stored. It is very difficult to understand why so little care or thought goes into the filing of information, because the result is that it is difficult or impossible to retrieve. It might as well have been thrown into the waste paper basket, if it cannot be found when you need it.

Another problem is in the form of the information itself. Most people, when producing letters or documents, think only of the immediate need. They forget that other people at a future date may need to read the document, and may be totally mystified by it. A few additional words to put things in context would make all the difference.

The application of groupware will not solve these problems. What it can do is help to develop a sensible framework that will help the flow and processing of information; provided of course that it is carefully introduced. Groupware will only work if the existing information flows within the office have been carefully studied, so that the new system can assist those areas where help is most needed, and where better or faster information will best benefit the aims of the organisation as a whole.

2.9 People have to change - but can they?

Even at the level of each individual office, the changes brought about by automation will be sometimes be unacceptable.

Anyone who has changed procedures in an office, for example, installing a new network system, developing a new filing system, moving from card files to a computer-based system, has experienced some resistance on the part of the people concerned. New methods and procedures require changes in the work habits of people, and some form of resistance is only to be expected.

Managers have been making changes in offices since offices began, for instance with the introduction of the typewriter or the telephone, although the changes have mainly been on a small scale. Each change brings some disruption to the office, but nothing so radical, we believe, as the kinds of changes that are called for by groupware technologies.

Thus, with a degree of wariness, we approach the subject of the groupware-enabled office. In its own way, it is the outward manifestation of a latter-day industrial revolution, with infinite capacity to make or mar the society which is its creator. Why then are so many organisations preparing to take this step? If they don't, they must realise that they will be unable to develop new ways of doing business and therefore their competitive edge will be lost.

2.10 The falling costs of equipment

One starting point is the falling cost of equipment and platforms. In the past ten years there have been revolutionary advances in the electronics industry, with spectacular cost reductions for components. There have been significant, if less spectacular, cost reductions in computers and office systems which use those components. If the reduction in cost and size and the improvement in performance of a memory chip, over the past 15 years, had been applied to a Rolls Royce motor car, it would now be available for £5, and be able to travel 18,000 miles to the gallon. The only disadvantage is that it would be the size of a thumbnail!

The cost of computer processors has tumbled over the past ten years: for a given level of performance, prices have fallen by 20 per cent per annum. This level of change is likely to continue over the next decade.

2.11 Salary costs

At the same time that equipment costs have been falling, the wages and salaries of office staff have been rising. The annual increase can be as high as 10 or 20 per cent.

<u>Contract of Employment</u>

Dear Prospective Employee

We would make you an offer of employment to fill the vacancy for which you applied. Your starting salary will be £7500. This may not appear to be a large amount but if you receive annual increases of 8%, work for us for 40 years, retire on half of your final salary and then live until you are 80, we will have invested £4 million in you.

Now that is a large amount!

Figure 2.4 The real cost of employing a white collar worker

The growth in the cost of administrative staff has even been accelerating in recent years. For example in many major cities, secretarial and typing staff salaries have trebled over the past decade.

This is during a period of economic depression. There is currently no indication that this rate of increase will slow down in the near future.

At these rates of increase, the investment a firm makes in each employee is substantial. Most people do not realise what kind of commitment they make when they employ an individual in an organisation. If we assume that someone is engaged at £7,500 per annum at age 25, works for 40 years, receives 8 per cent annual increases, retires at half his working salary, and lives to age 80, the total corporate commitment to that individual is £4 000 000. Every time an additional person is added to the staff, that is the kind of commitment a company makes! And it could, of course, still increase, depending on legislation, inflation, and many other factors.

And this is not the only cost. For every six people you need a supervisor, and there are overheads on top of salaries, so the total cost is quite staggering. That is one of the reasons why reengineering and groupware is being taken so seriously.

Chapter 3. Groupware requirements for 21st century business processes

3.1 No lists. Just directions

We are not in product sales and therefore we will not provide a list of groupware products and a glib description of some of their functionality. Neither will we suggest that all that needs to be done is to install these groupware packages in order to achieve the desired results. The value of these lists change with time and circumstances. Nor are we futurologists and therefore we do not propose to make forecasts about which software package will be the market leader and for how long.

For us, groupware is a range of facilities available from a range of products both hardware and software, the features of which are constantly changing. More importantly groupware is about the way in which these facilities may be applied when reengineering the business and its processes.

What is required is an understanding of the features and attributes of groupware and how they can be applied to create a more efficient and responsive organisation. Groupware will not be able to solve all of the problems in an organisation but, if sensibly applied, it will make a significant contribution. It is not the technology or the software package that needs to be examined but the way in which facilities offered by groupware can be applied to undertake activities in new and more effective ways.

3.2 Do not automate an inefficient activity - reengineer it

The fundamental error that most organisations commit when they look at technology is to view it through their existing processes. They ask how can we use these new technologies to enhance or streamline what we are doing already. Instead of how can we use technology to do things that we are not doing already. Reengineering, unlike automation is about innovation. Process reengineering is the means by which an organisation can successfully realise a significant improvement in performance, as measured in terms, for example, of service quality, cost-effectiveness or profitability. This is achieved by the application of a variety of tools and techniques which focus on the business as a set of related customer-oriented processes, rather than as a set of organisational functions.

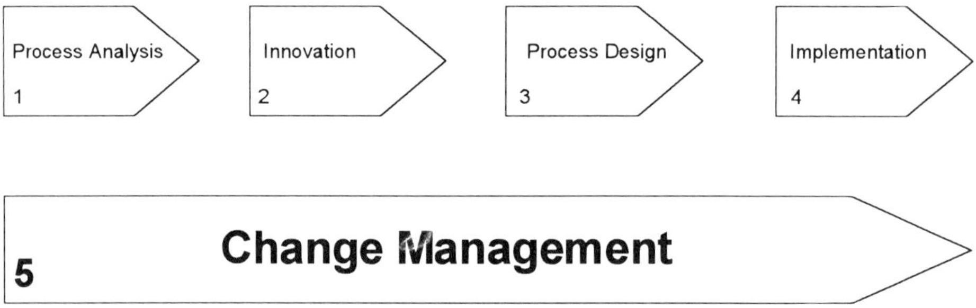

Figure 3.1 The five phases of change management

This is why groupware should not be mistaken for office automation. Groupware is the mechanism for changing the way in which we work. Reengineering is about exploiting the latest technology to achieve new goals. One of the more difficult aspects of re engineering a process is to recognising the new, unfamiliar capabilities of technology instead of its familiar ones. One has to find the new ways of working using previously unknown or unrecognised features of the technology.

To recognise the powers of technology and to visualise its application requires the use of a form of thinking that most business people do not learn and may feel uncomfortable using. Most white collar workers think deductively. That is that they are good at defining a problem or problems then seeking and evaluating different solutions to it. They are process-oriented in that they are focused on tasks, on jobs, on people, on structures but not on processes. But applying information technology to perform business reengineering demands inductive thinking - the ability to first recognise a powerful solution and then seek the problems it might solve.

3.2.1 Deductive thinking can miss the point

Thinking deductively about technology not only causes people to ignore what is really important, but it also gets them excited about the technology and the application that are in fact trivial. It is not the technology that is important it is how it is used. People who think technology rarely produce sustainable solutions A few years ago, an international organisation thought that the integration of the personal computer with the telephone would be a significant advance for the office automation arena. The unit would take up less space, be less expensive and could integrate these activities. That may be true but it did not offer a breakthrough in capability. It did not change the way in which processes were undertaken it just welded two technologies together. Once the marketing hype was reduced the 'All-in-one' did not make a sustained appearance on the market

A lack of deductive thinking about technology is not a new problem, nor is it confirmed to lay people. The All-in-one was designed and developed by a computer and telecommunications company. But that is not unusual, many of the computer companies have missed the implications and uses of technology. IBM missed the real power of the xerography and the photocopier machines. As far as they were aware it did not solve any known problems - if you want to copy a letter you use a copy ribbon in a typewriter or carbon paper. Anyway the traditional way of disseminating information was to send a memo with a circulation list so that everyone who needed to read the contents could do so - serially. The idea that an office would want to read it in parallel was not considered.

IBM also missed the true potential of the personal computer. It was a start up company, Apple, who started the exploitation of the personal computer. And even when IBM joined in, many other start up companies, helped by several small software companies, pushed the concept into directions inconceivable to anybody - least of all IBM.

What has to happen is that there is a need to think about the creative power of technology and work out how it will break the rules and allow a new order. There is a need to think beyond the restrictive limitations of paper.

3.3 Business processes have been structured by the limitation of paper

It is a sobering thought that the structure of our business processes have been structured by the limitation of paper. If information can only appear in one place at one time then work has to be managed serially - once the technology is available to provide data that can be viewed simultaneously the serial structure of work disappears.

Especially for an organisation that needs information to be displayed concurrently and allow a number of people to work on the same document or groups of information simultaneously.

3.3.1 Things need not always be the same

There is a need to think the unthinkable: restructure the normal rationale and accepted order; change the way in which activities are undertaken. There are many ways in which technology has changed the way in which tasks are undertaken. This will be included in groupware solutions.

The use of these technologies are explained in other parts of the book and include:

- **Video conferencing** provides the facility to 'meet' with colleagues and customers without travelling and disrupting a schedule
- **Teleworking** (working from home) with the use of WAN and powerful personal computers
- **Expert systems** allows if used creatively generalists to do complex tasks
- **Decision support** tools provide the facility to allow non-managers to make decisions

- **Workflow management software** ensures that there is a constant queue of work waiting to be processed, and once completed the work is routed to the next appropriate person or process station
- **Wireless communication system** provides instant access to the corporate system the minute it is switched on
- **Information highways** which allow all forms of information to be communicated to and from any linked location
- **Presentation technology** that allows an overhead slide display to be controlled directly from a palmtop computer.

These are a few examples of the way in which technology can enable new ways of working. Groupware is an amalgam of these linked together by a unifying infrastructure and enabled by the process of business reengineering.

As an essential enabler in the reengineering process, modern information technology has an importance that is difficult to overstate. But companies need to beware of thinking that technology is the only essential element in reengineering. Groupware is more than the technology, it will be a way of life for the 'office' workers of the latter half of the 1990's and the 21st century.

Section II. Introduction to groupware

Chapter 4. Groupware - what's that?

The office environment has changed dramatically over the past few decades thanks to the introduction of more and more new technology, new management procedures and organisational restructuring. As the commercial world becomes increasingly competitive and businesses strive to achieve maximum productivity and improved customer service, white collar workers have had to better themselves continually in order to prove their worth. In many offices, this has put enormous strain on the employees who have been forced to adapt rapidly to a more technical environment, which may have been introduced without adequate change or benefits management.

The mass introduction of the PC in the 1980s changed office culture significantly as workers became more 'self sufficient'. They suddenly had their own rich set of personal tools which could be used to improve their productivity and maintain their own personal repository of information. Recently, the Local Area Network (LAN) has caused yet another culture shock - information is no longer personal, communication capabilities have increased and workers are being organised into teams, empowered with the information and authority needed to achieve specific business objectives.

This office revolution has led to the average white collar worker:

- performing most of their daily tasks with the aid of a PC and associated software packages
- observing a rise in their personal productivity with the introduction of increasingly sophisticated office technology
- having to become more flexible and adaptable to change

- being under more scrutiny from managers as the business world becomes more competitive
- operating in a team, with more personal responsibility in achieving specific aims
- giving up their information privacy - with information sharing a priority, employees can no longer hold business information for themselves.

Even with all these changes, largely brought about by the widespread adoption of Office Automation technology, one aspect of office life which does not appear to have changed a great deal is the way in which people interact with one another. It could be argued that the introduction of electronic mail and other messaging systems has made face-to-face interaction a thing of the past. It is our experience that workers would still rather use the telephone or go downstairs to talk to somebody than communicate via electronic means. We commonly hear statements such as:

> "I hate this new voice mail thing. Whenever it comes on, I just put the phone down - I'm not going to spend all day talking to a computer".

There are a number of reasons for this with the main ones being:

- humans are sociable and enjoy communicating face-to-face with fellow employees. This form of social interaction is lost with communication via electronic means
- electronic communications are largely asynchronous. When a message is sent, it will, hopefully, be received immediately but there is no telling when the recipient will actually read or listen to the message. Indeed, unless the receiver explicitly replies, there is usually no way of telling if the message has been read and it is impossible to tell if the information has been digested. This functionality deters users from exploiting electronic messaging to the full
- without the two-way interaction experienced in face-to-face conversations, it is difficult to communicate the complex issues that require questioning to be fully understood
- electronic messaging systems are generally introduced into an organisation without adequate user support or 'benefits

management'. This results in users being unaware of the full functionality of the system, not understanding the benefits that it can bring to them and at the extreme, not even being aware that the facility exists.

Groupware is set to remedy this situation and perhaps cause the greatest multi-dimensional shift in office culture since the introduction of the personal computer or coffee machine! It will not only cure the problems of communication but will also enable effective cooperation and collaboration between employees by proactively supporting the team environment.

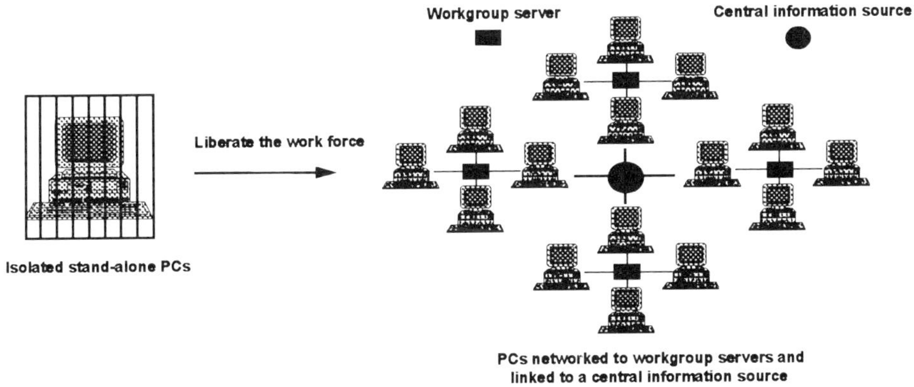

Figure 4.1 The move from isolation

The entry of groupware into an organisation requires considerable planning and careful management if it is to be widely accepted by the user population. Rushing in this new technology without adequate user support or involvement will ultimately lead to unsatisfactory results or can at worst end in disaster.

4.1 The importance of information?

One of the biggest drivers behind the introduction of groupware is its ability to allow information to be shared freely throughout an entire organisation. The importance of information as a business resource is finally becoming apparent and many people now believe whole heartedly that: 'information is useless until it is shared'.

4.1.1 What constitutes information

It is all very well to talk about information, but what is it actually? The simplest definition is that information is 'useful data'; with useful perhaps better described as being meaningful. An example of this is a telephone directory. It contains an abundance of data which only becomes information when you have a specific requirement. If you want to find the telephone number of a particular person, the entry for this person becomes information because it fulfils your requirement. If you turn this around and want to look for the person with a particular telephone number, this requirement is virtually impossible to fulfil because of the way data is organised. In this situation, the telephone directory remains as purely an abundance of data.

This scenario may appear to be completely irrelevant but it highlights a major problem in almost all offices - a lot of data is stored in filing cabinets and archived in warehouses under the misapprehension that it is information. In fact, approximately 90 per cent of all business information is held in this way with the rest being handled electronically. Most of the information stored in paper form is rarely used because of the way that it is organised - it's basically inaccessible. Unarchiving information can take days and even then there is no guarantee that the correct information will come back.

The problem of inadequate information management within organisations is highlighted in a survey that was carried out in 1992 by Touche Ross. They investigated a cross section of British companies and discovered that:

- 60 per cent of staff do not have the right amount of information to do their job properly and to their maximum potential
- this figure reduces to under 30 per cent in some larger organisations which have information management strategies in place.

As companies strive to manage themselves along multiple dimensions and cope with the business demands of the future, the importance of collecting, validating and disseminating information is becoming even more apparent. For this reason, more and more information will have to be handled and managed electronically if the figure of 60 per cent is to be reduced to an appropriate level.

4.1.2 Who needs information?

Everybody within an organisation needs access to information.

White collar workers need access to information from a variety of sources to perform their immediate job function. As they usually form the first line of customer contact, immediate access to the right information is essential to maintain an adequate level of customer service. Easy access to the necessary information is also required to maintain employee morale and to reduce the frustrations caused by 'information searching' activities. It would be interesting to estimate the total amount of time that the average white collar worker spends searching for information on a daily basis. We think that most managers would be both surprised and alarmed at the results. Providing access to a well organised corporate information base (the 'organisational memory') would enhance worker productivity and morale.

Middle managers need access to the information pertaining to their particular area of responsibility within a business to allow them to monitor performance and progress, to enable them to make changes to increase efficiency and also to plan for the future. This information may come from a number of sources and must be presented in a uniform and easily understood way.

Senior management need a company-wide view of performance and progress which will involve collating the information from all sectors of the business and presenting it in a uniform way. Maintaining an organisational memory will make the process of collecting and analysing this information much more simple and efficient.

It is therefore apparent that business information needs to conform to the following three requirements:

- stored - information needs to be stored in an electronic form so that it can be easily managed and is quickly accessible to those who need it. This is best achieved by creating a corporate database or organisational memory that is well organised and easily maintainable (document management systems)
- shared - information is useless until it is shared. Everybody within a company will benefit from a total information sharing culture; workers will become more knowledgeable and have fast access to

all the information they require (joint authoring, electronic messaging, information sharing tools)

- sifted - the large amount of information that will exist in an organisation is obviously not relevant to everybody. The average worker will only want to see a very small subset of the total corporate database and will not be concerned with the rest. A process of 'information irrigation' is required to take the information from a central pool and establish a framework to route it to the people who need it, when they need it (workflow management software, electronic messaging).

4.1.3 Legacy of information management

Information is widely considered to be the life blood of any organisation and without it, a business cannot function. This is true whether the organisation be office based or not - all businesses need access to customer information.

The problem that has faced so many organisations over the years is that information is probably the most important business resource but is also the most difficult to manage. Information comes in so many formats and from so many sources that, until now, it has been impossible to maintain a central, controlled repository of corporate data that everybody within the company has access to. Instead, many organisations have issued the task of information management at the departmental or some other level and are now faced with a number of isolated databases, residing on disparate machines, located on remote sites, sitting on different platforms and with no uniform or compatible communications system. Information is thus stored in a variety of formats and in a variety of places:

- in corporate, group and paper filing systems
- in corporate archives
- in corporate databases on mainframes
- on individuals' PCs in uncontrolled formats
- in the heads of certain employees.

With information stored in this way, access to particular material is limited to those people who know where it is. This is obviously not an ideal situation as business information is needed by all levels of management and by all employees within an organisation. This situation is widely known as the 'legacy of information management' and is currently inhibiting the business progress of many companies.

Groupware, along with the enabling hardware technologies, can provide a solution to this extremely common problem which is fast becoming the most demanding of business issues.

> "Freeing up data access and sharing business information more democratically across the organisation is probably the most pressing imperative for corporate IT managers today" [*Wright 1992*].

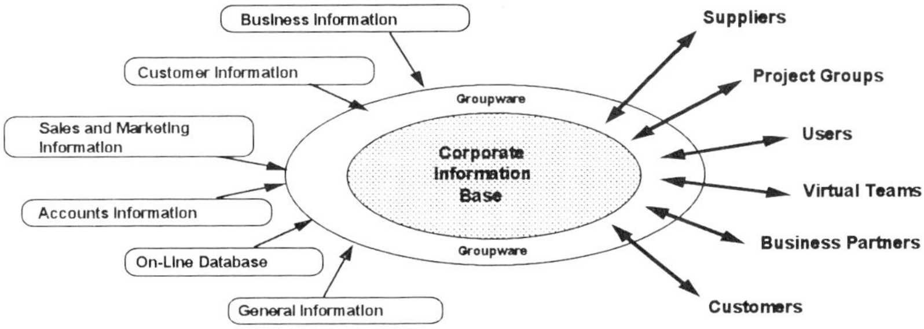

Figure 4.2 Creating the Organisational Memory

Many people would consider that groupware is the most sensible way to distribute information as deeply and widely throughout an organisation as possible, while retaining the endless possibilities for customising the presentation and analyses of that data at the individual, departmental and corporate levels.

4.1.4 The information life cycle

The importance of information and the frequency of its use will decline as it gets older and more out-of-date. This relationship is known as the information life cycle and consists of three stages:

- Childhood - in the childhood stage, information is used frequently as it is likely to represent the source for customer interaction, perhaps in the form of a new application form, or for reporting purposes, e.g., this month's sales figures. In a traditional information management system, information in the childhood stage would probably be held in paper form prior to the 'data entry'.

In childhood, information is produced by clerical staff and captured in the form of post, fax and data entry.

- Middle Age - once the information has been used initially, its relevance will begin to decline. In the traditional systems, middle aged information will be held in some form of local database or transaction processing system which is not accessible to everybody. In middle age, information is processed, tracked and distributed.
- Old Age - once information no longer becomes useful on a regular basis, it is archived. Paper documents are sometimes required to be kept for legal reasons and these are archived into warehouses. Digital information is archived onto cheap, high capacity magnetic storage media. Once information is in this state, it is difficult to retrieve in a limited time period. Groupware, along with the enabling technology of Document Image Processing (DIP), will allow all documents to be stored electronically and subsequently archived on to high capacity optical media. In this form, the information remains readily available at all times.

These stages can be represented diagramatically and are shown in figure 4.3 along with the storage methods that may be used in 'Groupware Information Management Systems'.

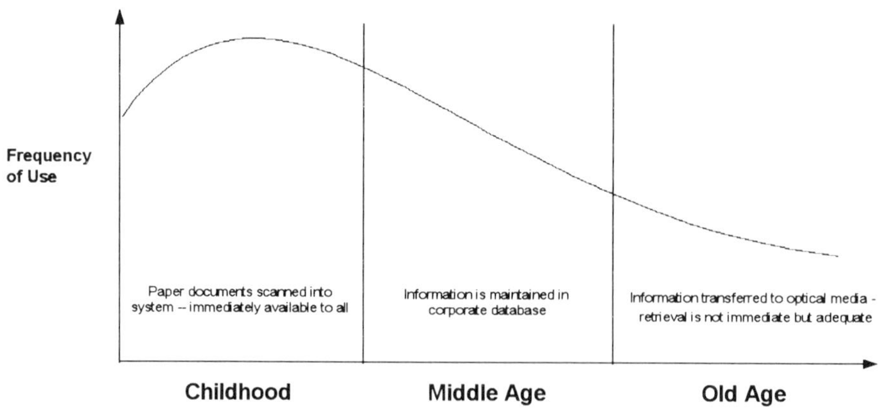

Figure 4.3 The information lifecycle

Groupware and the enabling hardware technologies of Document Image Processing and Computer Output to Laser Disc (COLD) can enable information to remain readily accessible throughout its entire lifecycle. This provides the potential for the creation of a total information sharing environment.

4.1.5 Problems of information management

Managing information so that it is storable, sharable and siftable does not come without its problems:

- not everybody wants to share their information - it may be regarded as private or may potentially damage an employee's reputation or position within the organisation
- divulging job specific information may give away the things that make a person indispensable to the company, therefore employees are not always willing to share it
- the correct IT and corporate infrastructure must be in place to allow everybody appropriate access to a central repository of business information
- you have to know what information a person or team needs and this will vary considerably from person to person, team to team and will also vary over time
- creating an information sharing environment means changing the culture of an organisation
- the repository of data, which is likely to be huge, has to be adequately maintained.

Among other things, groupware is a means by which this kind of information management can be achieved in an organisation.

> "It really has been useful, this sharing of information by computer. Now I hear about things quickly that before I used to hear about only by accident down the pub" [*Middle manager from the winning company in the 1991 Lotus Groupware Competition*].

4.2 A definition of groupware

Groupware is a term covering such a wide and ever expanding area that a definitive, all encompassing definition is almost impossible to derive. Many of the delegates at the first groupware conference in 1992 came away from it still unable to provide a short and precise description of the term. The components of groupware are so diverse that market research firms are unable to determine the size of the market, although most agree that groupware will comprise the largest IT market at the beginning of the next century.

Many people have attempted to define groupware but none of the definitions that we have encountered have succeeded in capturing the real essence of the groupware concept. The lack of such a definition may account for the enormous amount of confusion which currently surrounds the area. This point is highlighted in a survey conducted by PA Consulting Group during the latter part of 1993. Senior managers were interviewed from 100 organisations operating in diverse market sectors and 66 per cent of the respondents had either not heard of groupware or did not fully understand what the term referred to - some thought it was merely a fad word and others thought it was simply networking.

4.2.1 The evolution of groupware

Groupware evolved from the early work carried out in the field of Computer Supported Cooperative Work (CSCW). This area of research began in 1984 when Irene Greif and Paul Cashman decided to use the term CSCW to describe a particular workshop they were running. The intention of this workshop was to outline people's concerns about supporting a number of users working together with computer systems.

Research into CSCW is still continuing on a massive scale and a number of research projects are outlined in the book "CSCW" by Paul Wilson [*Wilson 1991*] and in the DTI's CSCW Awareness Initiative [*DTI 1994*]. Paul Wilson describes CSCW as:

> "a generic term which combines the understanding of the way in which people work in groups with the enabling technologies of computer networking and associated hardware, software, services and techniques".

Supporting individuals in their desire to work as a cohesive unit is the main essence of the groupware concept. This involves providing not only the software to enable effective team working but also the organisational framework in which teams can operate to their maximum potential. Business restructuring and process reengineering are an integral part of this process and the move to a groupware environment.

In addition to fulfilling the need to work in teams, groupware also evolved out of the need to:

- give more autonomy to the work force - in recent years, employees have been demanding a greater degree of autonomy in their work. This is especially true of those engaged in knowledge work. They want to have control of their day-to-day activities and ultimately have a significant influence on their destiny. Providing such autonomy involves giving workers the information, authority, responsibility and framework they need to carry out their tasks to the best of their ability. It also requires flexible working procedures and tools that can be tailored to individual ways of working. Groupware can deliver the prerequisites to increased autonomy through information sharing, increased communication and flexible tools which can be readily customised to individual preferences
- overcome the barriers created by time and space - organisations operating on a world-wide scale do not want to be inhibited by distance or time. Teams should be able to function regardless of where their members are located and the time zones they are operating in. By providing sophisticated messaging and electronic meeting capabilities, groupware provides this capability
- create an organisational memory - all the information a business needs to operate should be held in a central database, accessible to all. It must be capable of holding vast quantities of data in both structured and unstructured form. This involves text, image, video, sound and any other multi-media objects that may come to exist. The information needs to be readily available when and where it is needed. Groupware can provide document management systems to maintain the corporate memory and information routing and reporting tools to distribute it throughout the organisation
- be more responsive to change - as the business world becomes increasingly competitive and sophisticated technology becomes more widely available, gaining competitive advantage through IT or any other means is a difficult task. Instead, businesses will have to compete by being the first in a new field, the first to adopt new techniques and by being able to adapt rapidly to market changes

without losing efficiency or staff morale. Such endeavours are high risk but the potential benefits are enormous. Introducing groupware can give an organisation a leading technological edge and create a more responsive and adaptable business in the process.

4.2.2 What groupware is not

In deriving a definition of groupware, it is perhaps appropriate to begin by describing what groupware is not. This will also help to dispel some of the myths generated by some of the inaccurate descriptions of groupware given in the computing press.

Groupware is not just another buzz word invented by software and hardware suppliers in an attempt to coerce clients into buying the same products under a different name. Groupware is a whole new breed of software products designed to support a team working culture and is also a whole new way of thinking about corporate organisation. If groupware is used properly, its introduction can result in dramatic improvements in a number of crucial business areas.

Groupware is not merely networking of PCs with some shrink-wrapped software placed on top. Most networks are established for reasons of cost effectiveness: expensive peripherals can be shared, electronic communication is cheaper and faster, maintenance tasks can be standardised and centralised and so on. Discovering a user-oriented network that has been established primarily to support individuals and teams in their daily activities is surprisingly rare. Groupware aims to redress this balance and convert purely cost-oriented network installations into user-facing ones as well. These will concentrate on:

- better management of information flow through the office
- better sharing of tasks by allowing collaboration between colleagues
- better information sharing leading to enhanced customer service - everybody has access to the information they need
- better support for team working by providing sophisticated communication and co-working facilities.

General multi-user systems are not groupware. Simple multi-user systems do not make any distinctions between users and their varying requirements; all users are presented with the same tools through the same central system. Groupware understands that there are different kinds of user that require different views of the data at different times and in different places. A groupware solution will and should include a family of products whose whole will support the needs of every individual and team.

Groupware is not just an extension of traditional office automation systems. In traditional OA systems, applications are maintained on a central machine with access provided largely through dumb terminals but sometimes through PCs. This restricts the user to working with the set of applications offered by the OA package and does not allow the use of best of breed products. This is also true of modern office automation products such as Microsoft Office, Lotus Smartsuite and WordPerfect Office. With a groupware solution, best of breed products can be selected and because of the general support for open systems, they are easily linked together. Another distinction is that OA systems are more individually oriented - they give minimal support to those users who wish to work together. Groupware products are designed specifically for this purpose.

4.2.3 What groupware is

Paul Wilson states that groupware differs from CSCW in that it is more technology oriented. He argues that CSCW is more concerned with analysing the behaviour of workers and how they should be organised and educated to prepare them for the introduction of technology. We agree with this to a large extent but would say that a groupware implementation also includes the analysis of organisational structure and culture and how this must be changed and managed in order for it to be successful.

Some of the definitions of groupware that have previously been given are:

- co-evolving human tool system [*Englebart 1988*]
- intentional group processes and procedures to achieve specific aims with software tools designed to support and facilitate the group's work [*Johnsen-Lenz 1982*]

- computer-based systems that support groups of people engaged in a common task (or goal) and that provide an interface to a shared environment [*Ellis 1991*]
- groupware is the use of computer hardware and software to make the implementation of a business strategy based on teamwork and collaboration both easier and more productive [*Apricot 1993*]
- before businesses can exploit all of the benefits groupware has to offer, there needs to be a cultural revolution in the workplace [*Wright 1992*].

All of these definitions concentrate on the team or the group and how groupware provides the framework in which they can operate more effectively. They also mention the information sharing properties of groupware and the processes, procedures and culture change that must take place for groupware to be successful.

We believe that groupware covers such a diverse area with ever increasing boundaries that the best definition of groupware is an amalgamation of the following points:

- groupware is not an IT dominated area but is the result of the **integration** of many **academic and business fields** alike
- groupware is the response to **new management cultures** which emphasise the importance of **team working**
- groupware is a **family of electronic tools** which support individuals in their desire to work effectively together - it encourages team work rather than individualism
- groupware **augments human abilities** rather than attempting to replace them
- groupware is an **enabler** for organisations to examine and subsequently **redesign their business processes**
- groupware operates across **a number of dimensions** which must be analysed before implementation
- the introduction of groupware will **change the way people work** and the **redefine the cultures** present in many organisations - the interactive or interpersonal dimension of groupware is its key element.

Not just an IT dominated area

Groupware is the amalgamation of many disciplines from the academic and business worlds including distributed systems, human/computer interaction, artificial intelligence, social theory, psychology and management sciences. All have an interest in groupware because it is not just enabling technology but is a whole new way working. It requires those implementing groupware systems to understand the dynamics of a group, how individuals interact with one another, how effective teams can be built and how group processes can be supported using the available technology.

Computer supported cooperative working and groupware represent large research areas in the academic world. Researchers are interested in how the introduction of groupware affects organisational structure and culture and many are trying to provide models which can simulate this transition and thus allow organisations to plan ahead.

Researchers at Rank Xerox's Europarc in Cambridge are using a new approach, ethnomethodology, which has been designed to help them understand how people and technology interact at work [*Peltu 1992*]. Ethnomethodology considers the range of relationships between individuals, groups, work practices and technologies. This makes it very useful in examining the organisational impact of IT.

A response to new management cultures

Organisations are slowly beginning to realise that their employees along with factors such as effective management, marketing ploys and cost reduction, are the keys to business success. The collective knowledge of a work force is huge and usually remains untapped because of strict and rigid working procedures and controls. If these controls can be removed and a framework put in place whereby knowledge can be shared and views aired, significant benefits can be realised. This has recently been experienced in the car industry where many manufacturers have experienced substantial cost savings after implementing suggestions made by lower echelon employees working day-to-day on the business processes.

Organisations are also beginning to realise that it will require the collaborative efforts of interdisciplinary teams to continue producing innovative and market leading products in the future. This requires a team working culture to be established where teams can be established and then be disbanded as required. A groupware implementation brings with it a number of factors which can assist in the process of adopting a team environment:

- Connectivity - groupware permits group wide communication
- Control - groupware allows group control over process monitoring
- Collaboration - groupware encourages the sharing of data to maximise benefits
- Coordination - groupware can be used to coordinate the activities of a group to achieve common aims
- Change - groupware provides the opportunity for business processes to be analysed and subsequently reengineered to remove inefficiencies and adapt them to a team oriented scenario.

A family of electronic tools

It is important to understand that a groupware solution will generally consist of a set of tools or products used together rather than independently - it is the case where the whole is greater than the sum of the parts. One product will probably not be sufficient to cope with the needs of each work group as these will vary according to abilities of team members and the functions that they are performing.

Groupware products must be chosen to fit in with the way in which a team works and the processes in which it is involved. It is of no benefit to try and force a work group to operate according to the regime of one product - groupware must fit the processes and characteristics of a work group and not vice-versa. The groupware products which do include more than one function or technology generally restrict the work group in the same way as office automation products in that best of breed tools cannot be used.

Augmenting human abilities

The implementation of groupware usually involves empowering teams of end-users. This means giving the users the information and authority they need to carry out their function without the need for close supervision or management. It does not provide the user with a set of prescriptive rules which they must follow exactly but gives them the necessary framework in which they can carry out their tasks to the best of their ability. This usually involves the user adapting their particular environment to suit the way that they work.

> "Human judgement can never be fully replaced by technology. Instead, the technology will free us to do what only we can do. Groupware can support or hinder shared purpose, an atmosphere of trust and effective team working" [*Johnsen-Lenz 1992*].

In this respect, groupware augments human abilities rather than attempting to replace them.

An enabler for business process redesign

It has already been mentioned that groupware must fit the business process and not vice-versa. In order to achieve this aim, processes must be analysed to ensure that the most appropriate groupware product is chosen. This analysis provides the perfect opportunity to highlight the inefficiencies present in the processes and to subsequently eliminate or minimise these by redesign.

Business process reengineering has become a widely used term throughout this decade and companies have increasingly turned to this technique in the hope of streamlining processes and maximising efficiency. Many groupware products provide tools to assist in this activity.

Operating across a number of dimensions

A book on the subject of groupware would not be complete without mentioning the two dimensional groupware model designed by Robert Johansen. In this model, Johansen analyses the various categories of groupware depending on whether the participants are interacting in the same or different places at the same or different time.

This model is useful in grasping the concepts of groupware, i.e., that it is an enabler for individuals to communicate, collaborate and cooperate regardless of time and place, but we believe that it is far too simplistic. There are many more dimensions to groupware that can affect the technology that is employed, e.g., the structure of the information being processed, the degree of user autonomy, the adaptability of users to change, the sources of the information, etc.. These dimensions will be analysed further in section III when we describe how to match the characteristics of your work groups to the available technologies.

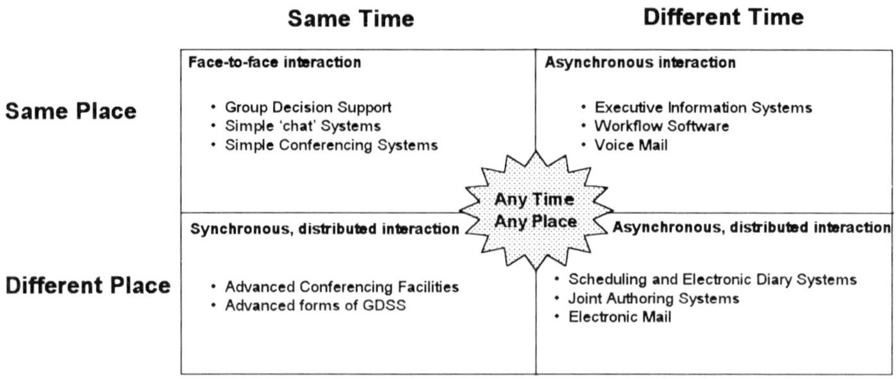

Figure 4.4 The Johansen model

Changing the way people work

The introduction of groupware will change the way that people work. It will require them to work in groups which operate in a flat management structure in an environment where information is shared freely across the entire organisation. The reasons for this change and the transformation in organisational culture which will accompany it are examined further in section III.

4.2.4 Why groupware has taken off

With Douglas Englebart designing what could be classed as the first groupware applications over 30 years ago, why has it taken this long for groupware to really catch on in the market. The main reason for this is that the gap between the demand for the services that groupware can bring and the technology that is needed to bring those services has grown increasingly smaller.

The technology for groupware

To facilitate a groupware implementation, users must have access to a PC that is networked with those in their immediate work group if not those of the entire organisation. An easily accessible, central repository of corporate information is useful to facilitate the necessary data sharing and an electronic messaging system is required to form the basis for communication. The technology of the underlying network must be such that it provides a reliable medium for rapid data delivery and should allow all forms of multi-media data to be passed along it.

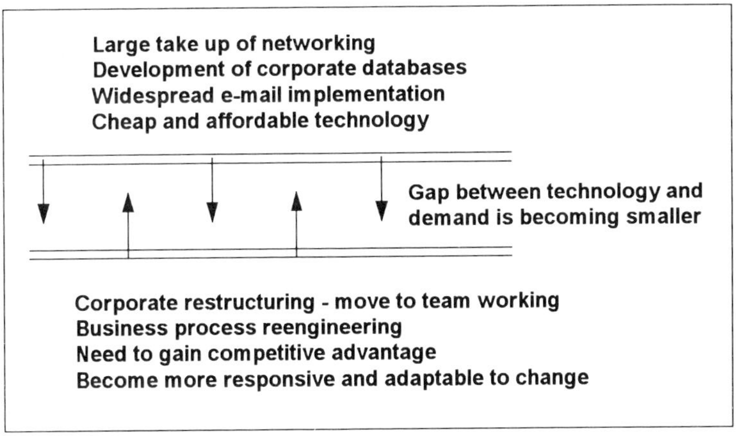

Figure 4.5 The demand for groupware

In the past few years all of the above mentioned technology has become available at very affordable prices. This has led to a large take up of PC networking in organisations with the subsequent addition of messaging and multi-media facilities. It is predicted that by 1995, over 60 per cent of the 100 million PCs worldwide will networked [*Shephard 1992*] with the number of e-mail users expected to rise by a staggering 60 per cent.

The big drive towards open systems and client-server architectures has also helped groupware to gain a significant foothold in the market. Section V concentrates on these issues and describes the architecture and infrastructure which is necessary for a successful groupware implementation.

The demand for groupware

It is a well known fact that the amount invested in IT by organisations over the past two or three decades has not been adequately rewarded by tangible business benefits such as improved worker productivity or a reduction in costs. It has been shown that white collar productivity may not increase at all or by percentages as small as 0.7 per cent even when large IT investment has been made.

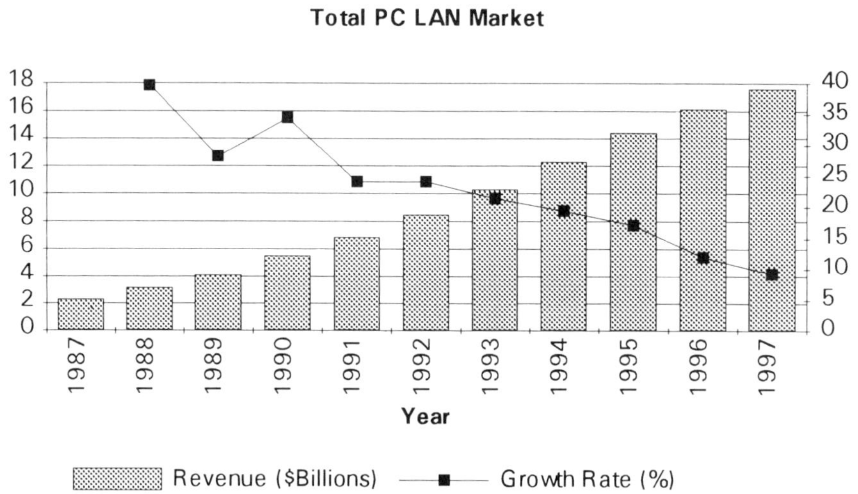

Figure 4.6a The Increase in the LAN Market

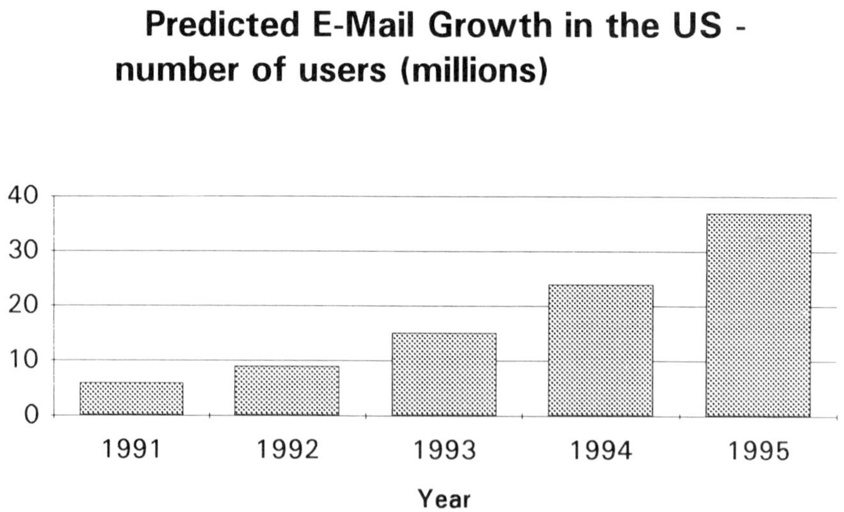

Figure 4.6b The increase in the use of E-mail

This is in stark contrast to the manufacturing industry where productivity improvements have been known to reach 70 per cent. A recent report by the Massachusetts Institute of Technology concluded that the return on IT investment is improving over time because organisations are more willing to integrate the investment with radical reforms in business processes and organisational structure and culture.

The reason for the success of the manufacturing industry may be attributable to the way that workers are organised. This is primarily in teams, all with a specific objective and the necessary tools to achieve that aim. Many businesses outside of manufacturing are now beginning to realise that individuals do perform better in teams where ideas are shared, help is given by colleagues, a friendly, supportive atmosphere is created and employee morale is high. The emphasis is now on creating flatter management structures where workers are organised into teams and empowered with the necessary tools and information to carry out a business process.

Groupware is an enabler for this transformation which not only increases worker productivity but in the process of forming groups, the organisation has an opportunity to review its business processes and change these for the better. Business process reengineering is the common term for this procedure and its current prominence in the business world is partly due to the success of the many groupware products which enable it to effectively take place.

Other drivers behind the increased demand for groupware are:

- to try and reverse the trend of high IT spend with little reward
- the belief that sharing corporate information is vital for business success
- to overcome the limitations of time and space - to be able to communicate and collaborate 'any time, any place'
- to create a more responsive organisation
- groupware is held in high acclaim and a groupware implementation gives an organisation a prestigious appearance
- those organisations which have successfully implemented groupware have reported a range of phenomenal benefits including increased productivity, cost savings, better customer service, increased employee morale, more adaptability to changes in the market place and greater communication with the outside world.

4.3 The groupware dream

Groupware and the issues surrounding it are set to revolutionise human behaviour both in the office place and in every day life. The prospect of advanced communication facilities becoming widely available, teleworking becoming more popular, organisations adopting a flatter, network management structure and employees being organised into teams will have a dramatic effect on the lives of many individuals.

The advent of groupware makes the future an even more interesting and exciting proposition. It also makes speculative visions of the future more difficult as so much may change. Such visions of the future need to be made in an attempt to identify potential problems and thus prepare for these.

One thing that can be certain about the future is that the use of electronic information will become increasingly widespread. In an article entitled 'Groupware in the 21st Century', Geoff Vincent of PA Consulting Group predicts that this increased use of electronic information will change the way we behave and the way we think. He says that it will alter work patterns and lifestyles. It will change the way we relate to friends, family and colleagues - bringing some people closer together and driving others further apart. It will inevitably affect our mental picture of the world which means that it will change what we perceive as reality.

This may appear to be far fetched but with the amount of reliance that we place on information both personally and in business, as information changes, so will we. In organisations, power and status are often based on access to and control of information. When information is freely available to anybody who wants it, what will happen to those in authority. Their roles will obviously change from being controllers and guardians of information to ones where they concentrate on managing information flows. Alternatively they may disappear completely.

In this section, we present a speculative vision of the future by describing what the average day of an office worker might be in the 21st century. This may of course be completely irrelevant if technology and culture change to the extent where offices become a thing of the past.

4.3.1 The 21st century office worker

Paul Williams bolts down the flight of stairs leading to platform 1 and just makes it onto the 7.33 train bound for London's Victoria station. The train is overcrowded as usual and Paul is extremely glad that he only has to make this journey to the office every now and again. As the train pulls away from the station, Paul remembers what it was like in the 1990s when he had to go to the office every day. The office then was enormous - a four storey building in the centre of London housing over 600 staff and costing the company an extortionate amount of money every year. He used to enjoy the social aspect of meeting his colleagues every day but with the advanced **video conferencing** facilities in his home he still has the capability of 'meeting' with colleagues whenever he pleases.

Today, the company office comprises of only a single floor most of which is devoted to housing the large number of corporate computer servers and the conference rooms where clients who have refused to adapt to the culture of **electronic meetings** are entertained. It is for the latter, that Paul is travelling to the office today, to meet one of his clients. Paul works for Long Life Assurance, a large life assurance and pensions company, and is a member of the team which has the responsibility for dealing with the company's corporate pensions offering. The client he is meeting today wants to discuss how his company can access Long Life's computer systems to give his employees the chance to check on the state of their individual pension schemes. Creating **'organisational memories'** is now a business priority and Paul has had many similar meetings in recent times. Long Life (LL) welcomes this access because it has significantly reduced the number of customer enquiries being made in this area. Also LL is attempting to create close partnerships with its clients - as everybody now realises, successful partnerships lead to business success!

With the vast and continual improvement of communication links since the 1990s, many companies have taken the same steps as Paul's to reduce the cost of office space, by allowing employees to work from home. **'Teleworking'** (working from home) started to gain popularity towards the end of the 1990s but really took off with the development of the **information superhighway** which now allows all forms of information to be communicated to and from households. Paul is provided with all the facilities that he needs to complete his tasks, which he does in significantly less time at home without the distractions of the office. It also allows him to spend more time with the children. The **workflow management software** that has been implemented throughout his team means that he constantly has a queue of work waiting for his attention and once he completes his stage, the work is routed to the next appropriate person.

From his portable computer at home, Paul has access to all the computer systems that he needs and with the **advanced messaging** and **joint authoring** facilities provided to him, he can communicate more efficiently with his colleagues than if he were working in an office with them. He doesn't even have to use a modem to 'dial in'; the **wireless communication system** means that he has instant access to the corporate system the minute he switches on.

Paul removes his pocket computer (palmtop) from his overcoat and checks the location and time of his meeting. He also takes the opportunity to check that the slides for his presentation are there and he flicks through them to ensure that he is fully prepared. He was pleased when LL invested in the new **presentation technology** that allows him to display overhead slides directly from his palmtop; he always used to get in a muddle with overhead transparencies.

As he is flicking through the slides, the familiar bleep from his palmtop and the appearance of Joanne's face on the screen tells him that his colleague has sent him a message. He pulls out his touch pen, and clicking on the smiling face of Joanne, begins to listen to her voice. Bad news! Joanne is ill and can't make the meeting this morning. Why are things so complicated, Paul thinks as he accesses his **electronic diary and scheduling** package to check who else is available to attend. He enters the time of the meeting and gets a list of colleague's names as a response. He selects Michael, who he hasn't seen for some time and who still lives relatively close to the office, and the meeting is automatically booked in Michael's diary.

(Paul's image appears on the screen of Michael's PC as he is sitting working at his desk at home. Michael reads the associated message in his diary. Michael has only got an hour to make it to the office!)

The train pulls in at a station and Paul sits down in one of the seats which becomes free. He reaches into his briefcase and takes hold of his portable computer. He turns it on and pulls up the pensions report that he has been working on with four of his colleagues. Immediately, he can see that Helen has made some changes to the management summary. This annoys him as he spent a lot of time on this but after reading the associated comments, he knows that the changes were necessary. LL invested in the **joint authoring software** as soon as it became available and since then Paul hasn't worked on a report or paper until two o'clock in the morning once; an activity which previously occurred with extreme regularity.

Flicking through the document, Paul also notices that some diagrams have been added. As he is studying the diagram on page 4, John inserts the paragraph he has been working on this morning into page 4and Paul's screen changes to incorporate the paragraph which John has just entered. Paul reads this with interest and makes some amendments to it.

John notices the amendments and is satisfied that they enhance the readability of his entry. Years ago, John would never have let somebody change his wording without a heated discussion The shift in culture that has taken place in the company over the past few years has changed his attitude though. He now realises that **effective team working**, **cooperation** and **collaboration** are the keys to achieving business success. Since the introduction of the **structural and cultural changes** within the organisation, LL has experienced many amazing benefits and John himself has seen an increase in his personal productivity and morale. This is partly due to being given the information, tools and authority necessary to carry out his function. He is no longer under the direct scrutiny of his manager, whom he now communicates with, via his PC, only once a week. He does realise that he is fortunate to be working for a company who planned and managed the change in structure and culture extremely well. Many of his friends, working in organisations where a similar transformation has been attempted, have become disillusioned with the new way of working with the result that the company's significant investment has achieved no benefits at all.

As the train pulls into Victoria station, Paul places his portable in his briefcase and makes his way to the office.

Paul sits down at one of the 'hot desks' available in the office and takes out his portable again. [Hot Desks is the term his company use for desks that anybody can use. With most employees now predominantly working from home, there is no longer the need to provide a desk for specific people except the company receptionists. Their role now mostly involves welcoming visitors - with most organisations using **electronic messaging facilities** for all forms of communications, there isn't much post to sort and the phone hardly ever rings.]

Looking at his watch, he realises that he has some time to waste, so he puts the morning newspaper disk into the disk drive and updates himself with yesterday's events. As he does so, he ponders on the peculiarity of this - reading yesterdays events in a newspaper when he has access, via the corporate computer systems, to up to the minute news via the **world-wide public information service**. He concludes that not all human habits can be changed immediately and anyway, he enjoys reading the paper - even if it is on a nine inch screen. He knows that eventually he will stop though.

He finishes reading the paper, and with the five minutes he has left, he decides to look at the company's current sales opportunities and the state of the cash flow. With all corporate information now available to everybody within the company, any employee can monitor the progress of LL's business. He runs the **executive information system** package and flicks through the series of graphs, tables, charts and diagrams which are displayed - so much easier to read than printed reports, he concludes. With this thought, it dawns on Paul that throughout most days of his working life, he now hardly ever touches a bit of paper. At home, paper is still in abundance - other members of his family are not very adaptable to change - but again, he knows that before long he will be forced to subscribe to the **local electronic information service**.

Being a forward thinking person, Paul welcomes change and sees this as the reason for his successful promotion within the company. The company's policy of **rewarding employees for group success** as opposed to solely for individual merit is the system Paul likes to operate in.

A flashing message on Paul's screen alerts him to the fact the Michael has arrived and that his clients are waiting in reception. With this, Paul makes his way to conference room six. He is looking forward to this session as it gives him the chance to use the new **electronic meeting facilities** and the **electronic brainstorming tool**. The reports on this tool have been very good, suggesting that people are less shy with the anonymity that is provided and therefore contribute more ideas and are more creative. He hopes that this is true.

After the meeting, which proved to be a great success, Paul returns home, glad in the knowledge that he will not be making the trip to the office again in the near future.

4.3.2 Could this be reality?

The answer to this is 'yes, it could'. The advances that are currently being made in the hardware and communications fields will provide the necessary framework on which appropriate software products can be developed.

Most of the scenario presented relied on the introduction of quite complex communications facilities. Communication links are getting better and more reliable all the time and wireless communications are already being used by some companies. The bandwidth of currently available links is sufficient enough to allow the passing of multi-media objects such as large text objects, for example, sound, video and image (commonly known as BLOBS - Binary Large Objects). As the available bandwidth continually increases, more forms of multi-media will be able to be communicated with greater reliability. 'Bandwidth on demand' services are becoming more widely available and as the information superhighway is put in place these services will become open to the average household.

The speed of CPUs is still following the trend of doubling every couple of years while remaining relatively stable in price. This is set to continue as we move from single processor systems to symmetric multi processor (SMP) and then to massively parallel systems (MPP). This will provide the necessary architecture to allow the type of applications mentioned in the description to be developed.

Most of the applications mentioned in the 'dream' are already available in some form or another but without the full functionality of those described. Messaging software is already widely available and implemented in many organisations. Some messaging applications provide an integrated messaging capability that allows facsimiles and other communications methods to be sent and received from the desktop. Intelligent mail applications are available that allow messages to be sorted or sifted according to certain criteria. This can help to overcome the information overload which often accompanies the introduction of electronic mail.

Video conferencing is becoming more popular as the technology becomes more widely available at reasonably affordable prices. Many products are now on the shelves including Fujitsu's Desktop Conferencing and Olivetti's Personal Communications Computer Kit. The expense of these systems and the poor quality of the pictures is still preventing their widespread take up.

Scheduling tools are currently available that allow meetings to be arranged without having to speak directly to the people involved. These tools also allow workers to check on the availability of their colleagues and to schedule resources such as meeting rooms and equipment. Advanced scheduling packages can be used to schedule the activities of a group project and to establish milestones which can be used to judge the progress.

Joint authoring is an area without much support at present. Being able to simultaneously work on the same document with amendments appearing on the screen in real-time is a tool which is not yet widely available. Most of the existing joint authoring tools assign certain parts of the document to different people. Only the owner of the section can amend it with others users having read access.

With relational database management systems (RDBMS) now capable of efficiently managing databases of up to 200Gb in size, creating and maintaining a corporate database is a realistic possibility. With the document management tools that are available, managing the location and distribution of this data is also possible. What is still lacking is the adequate integration of software tools with the RDBMS and multi-media objects.

Tools to allow data to be reported are widely available. Executive information system applications are quite sophisticated, being able to pull and standardise data from a number of disparate sources and display this in a user friendly and uniform way.

Group decision support systems (GDSS) provide a means for electronic meetings to take place. This means providing electronic brainstorming tools, electronic whiteboards and facilities for electronic voting. Most of these tools are available although they do not seem to be widely implemented as yet. The studies that have been performed regarding the impact of this technology are extremely promising, indicating that people react positively to GDSS. The anonymity that electronic meetings can provide tends to increase everybody's participation and groups are more likely to achieve consensus and commit to following through on action plans developed during a GDSS meeting.

The capabilities of case or workflow management systems are being exploited more and more by organisations which have a number of paper shuffling processes. In conjunction with document image processing, workflow software can be used to fully automate manual processes. The benefits reported by the companies that have successfully employed workflow techniques are impressive, with all reporting significant increases in productivity.

Once software has been developed to take advantage of the available hardware and communications facilities and to integrate multi-media capabilities, many of us may be experiencing the working life of Paul Williams in the next century. The main barrier to this will not be the technology required but will be the adaptability of people and organisations to change. Organisations will be forced to change their culture, structure, reward and promotion criteria and training programmes at the very least. Employees will have to respond positively to this change and be able to work in a team environment where they have more personal responsibility for achieving a business objective and all information is shared and accessible by all those who require it.

The planning and management of this transformation will be the key issue and will be the factor that will determine success from failure.

Chapter 5. The technologies of groupware

The groupware umbrella is huge and growing all the time. The last couple of years have seen a slow but steady emergence of PC based products designed specifically to support team working. These products, labelled as groupware, range from simple applications - sending documents between PCs - through more complex software - electronic diary and scheduling software - to full scale information management systems which provide a whole host of facilities designed to assist a team of individuals. The diversity of the products now falling under the groupware umbrella makes it impossible to analyse the market as a whole. Some form of segregation is required to assess the capabilities of the products in each sector and also to give the situations in which each category of technology is useful.

In the past, the groupware market has been segmented in a number of different ways. It has been:

- split into divisions by one of its many dimensions such as time and place. This leads to four categories of technology corresponding to the four squares of the Johansen model: any time, any place; any time, same place; same time, any place; same time, same place
- categorised into other dimensions such as the degree of the structure to the task and the information being processed or the degree of user autonomy and flexibility
- segmented into application areas such as sales management applications, product development and service applications, customer service applications and executive information system applications.

The most common form of segregation is by the different functions that the software can perform and we continue this trend by analysing groupware products under the following headings:

- Electronic messaging and conferencing
- Information sharing
- Electronic scheduling
- Case / workflow management
- Group decision support systems (GDSS)
- Reporting tools.

5.1 Electronic messaging and conferencing

Electronic messaging is the most familiar form of groupware and comprises all the software tools which enable electronic communication to take place. This is largely electronic mail but also includes desktop conferencing, video conferencing, desktop 'chat' facilities, voice mail and bulletin board systems. Some applications provide an integrated suite of desktop messaging facilities such as e-mail and facsimile.

5.1.1 Electronic mail

Electronic mail allows the asynchronous exchange of textual messages with some systems also supporting the exchange of multi-media objects. E-mail is analogous to sticking notes on a colleague's computer screen. Most systems include the ability to attach various documents, to maintain address lists, to reply to messages and to forward them on. Many other applications are now 'mail-enabled' which means that documents can be mailed from them directly.

Most people regard e-mail as simply an application but Eugene Lee of software vendor Beyond, stresses that e-mail is fundamentally an enabling technology. It is the foundation of work group computing that will slowly become the messaging infrastructure supporting a whole host of other applications such as multi-media mail, fax routing, database access, scheduling and document sharing.

The proliferation of e-mail systems into organisations has led to some experiencing the 'information overload' problem. Suddenly, employees are bombarded with messages and the efficiency which e-mail should bring is lost because of the time taken to work through these notes. Some e-mail packages have tried to combat this by including intelligence which can be used to filter only the important messages.

Voice mail has recently become popular in organisations and this facility provides employees with a personal answering machine that they can access from remote locations. Voice mail has the advantage that the only piece of technology required for people to leave messages is a normal telephone.

Electronic Mail Products	• Microsoft Mail • Lotus Development's cc:Mail • Beyond's Beyondmail • Multinational Software's Da Vinci for Windows • Finansa's Winmail.
Benefits	• enhanced communication throughout the organisation • the ability to transmit documents and other files to colleagues • support for remote workers who can keep in touch using e-mail • provides the foundation for the adoption of work group computing.
Disadvantages	• can cause information overload - facility is used to extremes with the result that employees spend atoo much time reading mail messages • security - the security of mail boxes and the fact that a document could inadvertently be sent to the wrong person or group of people. This has led to organisations specifying the types of document which can be transmitted via e-mail.

5.1.2 Conferencing

There are many different forms of conferencing products ranging from simple 'chat' facilities to full scale video conferencing systems that allow meetings to be conducted between people located at opposite ends of the globe.

'Chat' products allow two or more people to hold a real-time conversation from their PCs, perhaps from remote locations. Typically, the PC screen splits into segments with each segment representing the input of a particular participant. As words are typed, they automatically appear on the screen of all those involved in the conversation.

Desktop conferencing allows a number of people to hold a conversation or meeting in real time from their desktop computer. This can just be the real-time exchange of text or can involve video capabilities so that the image of each participant appears on the screens.

Conferencing Products	• Olivetti's Personal Communications Computer (PCC) kit • Northern Telecom's Visit • PictureTel's Live PCS 100 System • Fujitsu's Desktop Conferencing • IBM's Person To Person/2.
Benefits	• save on travel time and costs • establish closer relationships with customers and colleagues • provides an enabler for teleworking.
Disadvantages	• systems are currently expensive although prices are continually falling • picture quality is generally poor • current products have limited group conferencing abilities.

5.2 Information sharing

This is software which permits individuals residing at various locations to share information. In its simplest form, this is merely the efficient organisation of documents so that information can be found. In its complex form, this means providing simultaneous access to documents to facilitate multi-user editors or joint authoring capabilities.

5.2.1 Document management systems

Document management systems allow for the efficient organisation of documents and basically provide a complex 'file manager'. Typically, they remove the restrictions of directory and file names only having eight characters, they manage access rights to documents, they allow private and shared directories to exist, they control the backup, restore and archiving of documents and some provide free text retrieval facilities that can be used to perform complex searches.

Document Management Systems Products	• Quintec's SoftSolutions • Infostructures' Keyfile • PC Docs' PC Docs Open • Xsoft's Globalview.
Benefits	• efficient management of all forms of document irrelevant of location • automatic control of backup, restore and archiving • enhanced information sharing through ease of document location.
Disadvantages	• overhead due to document management database • may result in the use of long and complicated directory paths and filenames.

5.2.2 Joint authoring

Joint authoring systems and multi-user editors allow a group of people to jointly compose and edit documents. This prevents the need for one person to own the document until their section is complete, to pass it to the next person in the group for them to complete their bit and so on. The ideal joint authoring tool would allow the members of the group to access the document simultaneously, with amendments showing up in real-time. This requires complex software though and most systems do not provide this functionality. Instead they allocate sections of the document to individuals, with others in the group having read access but only the owner being able to amend it.

Some systems provide explicit notification of other user's actions, for example, a user will be informed if a portion of the document has been changed which directly affects the content of his or her portion. This is extremely useful when the document is a computer program.

Joint Authoring Products	• Access Technology's ForComment • Lotus Development's Notes • Rank Xerox's DocuTeam • DEC Teamlinks • ICL Teamware • Bull OfficeTeam.
Benefits	• encourages more integrated team work • speeds up document and report production • provides a means for comments to be attached during proof- reading.
Disadvantages	• 'pure' joint authoring requires extremely complex software • if write access is given to all authors for the entire document, a particular section may be amended several times by different people, ultimately leading to confusion • with authors having the opportunity to alter colleagues work, a document may actually take longer to produce but will be of higher quality.

5.3 Electronic scheduling

There is no advantage in building teams if the activities of team members cannot be coordinated or scheduled in some way. Electronic diary and scheduling packages provide this facility.

Personal organisers became essential tools in the chaotic business world of the late 1980s. Personal organisers were extremely useful in organising the daily lives of young executives but they provided no assistance for colleagues or secretaries who wanted to know the whereabouts or plans of certain employees. Electronic diaries and organisers are the 90s equivalent of the personal organiser. By maintaining an electronic diary, employees give their colleagues the facility to peer into their plans and know how they can be contacted.

Scheduling Products	• Microsoft's Schedule+ • Lotus Development's Organiser • European Software Publishing's Meeting Maker XP • WordPerfect's Office • Fischer International's Totally Automated Office (TAO).
Benefits	• meetings scheduled more efficiently with fewer subsequent cancellations • increased awareness of the location and plans of employees • effective scheduling of group's tasks.
Disadvantages	• only operates if diaries are maintained by all involved • not really appropriate for teams with members continually on the move.

Electronic schedulers are connected to the diaries and are used to automatically schedule meetings, resources and can be used to organise the activities of a group during a joint project. The scheduler uses the information provided in the diary to know when employees are free and therefore available for meetings, etc.. If everybody maintains their diary appropriately, the software can take a list of participants and schedule the meeting for the time and date when all are available, booking any of the necessary resources at the same time. Scheduling software is essential if a team is to operate as a truly cohesive unit.

5.4 Case / workflow management

Case or workflow software enables manual business processes to be automated. A classic example is the processing and approval of mortgages, where a sequence of actions and approvals are required, by different people, before the mortgage is granted or rejected. Workflow management systems use a model of the business process to ensure that data and documents follow the prescribed sequence of tasks and that users at each stage are provided with the information they need and are prompted for any data they must input.

Workflow Products	• Staffware's Staffware • Filenet's Workflo • Plexus' FloWare • NCR's ProcessIT • Bull's Flowpath • Workhorse Systems' Workhorse • ICL's Powerflow.
Benefits	• usually results in significant productivity gains • greater control of work flows • enabler for the reengineering of business processes • faster response times for what were paper-based activities
Disadvantages	• complete automation of a task takes away any degree of user autonomy • requires adoption of a whole new way of working.

Workflow management products originate from two main backgrounds. Firstly there are those products that have emerged from office automation and e-mail. These utilise a model of text messaging and the storing and forwarding of text documents. Other products have their origins in document image processing (DIP) and concentrate on the routing of image documents to users. Most products in the first category have subsequently had DIP integration added to them.

Many workflow applications are successful because they simplify and accelerate critical business processes that were previously constrained by paper-based activities.

5.5 Group decision support systems

Group decision support software provides computer-based facilities for the exploration of unstructured problems in a group setting. The goal is to improve the productivity of decision-making meetings, either by speeding up the decision making process or by improving the quality of the resulting decisions. Examples are electronic white boards, voting systems, brainstorming tools, idea organisation and issue analyses. It has been proven that the anonymity provided by these tools makes people less shy and more likely to contribute ideas with greater creativity.

GDSS Products	• Decision Dynamics's Teamworker • IBM's TeamFocus • Ventanna Corp.'s Group Systems • Collaborative Technologies Corporation's VisionQuest.
Benefits	• more focus in meetings leading to greater satisfaction • anonymity leads to greater participation and creativity - no one dominator • hard copy of the meeting is automatically provided • leads to shorter, more productive meetings.
Disadvantages	• group decisions support systems are currently expensive • a group facilitator is still required to coordinate the meeting • cultural change is required to adopt the electronic meeting tools.

Studies that have been performed to assess the benefits provided by these systems have concluded that people react positively to GDSS -

the participants involved actually enjoyed the meetings and looked forward to their next one! Participants also felt that they were more likely to reach a consensus and commit to following through on action plans developed in the meetings.

5.6 Reporting tools

As the amount of information within an organisation grows out of proportion, it becomes increasingly difficult for executives and senior managers to monitor business progress and analyse the information presented to them. This problem is escalated when information is stored in a variety of formats and in different locations. Reporting tools solve this by allowing selected information to be drawn from a number of sources and then reported in a uniform and user friendly way. This is the area of executive and management information systems.

Executive Information Systems (EIS) have become very fashionable in recent years and now sit on a number of senior managers' desktops, providing them with a detailed view of specific areas of the business. Many PC database packages now come with EIS type tools to allow efficient reporting of the data contained within them.

EIS Products	• Pilot's Lightship • European Software Publishing's Forest and Trees • SoftKlone's ShowBusiness • Gupta's Quest • IRI's PC Express • Comshare's Commander EIS.
Benefits	• increased access to fundamental business information • better presentation of detailed information • permits more informed decision making.
Disadvantages	• will probably require consistent tailoring to meet the changing information needs of senior managers • poor integration with multi-media objects such as sound and video.

5.7 Generic product facilities

When purchasing a groupware product or a set of products, there are certain generic facilities that should be offered regardless of which category of technology the software fits into. A product that offers all of the following facilities will offer the greatest degree of flexibility for future expansion and enhancements:

- Support for Version Control - with interaction occurring potentially at any time, any place and with any form of object being able to be communicated, it is essential that support for version control is provided. This enables people to know if objects have changed since they last accessed them. This could take the simple form of allowing comments to be attached to objects so that descriptions of changes could be given or could be provided by fully fledged configuration management control. **Does the product provide facilities for monitoring, combining and rationalising versions?**
- Access to distributed data locations - data will undoubtedly be stored in a number of disparate locations and in a variety of formats. The software must be capable of accessing data regardless of its form or location. **Does the product have facilities for managing both structured and unstructured data, stored in different locations?**
- Concurrent access - with information being shared and a high degree of collaboration between team members, it will be necessary for objects to be accessed simultaneously. **Can a number of people access and update an object simultaneously with all amendments being seen by a all participants in real-time?**
- Physical location independence - information and people are likely be spread over wide areas. **Can the product be used regardless of the location of the person using it?**
- Built-in intelligence - the amount of information available is increasing all the time and it is becoming more important to be able to filter this information. **Can the product have intelligence built into it to aid in the process of filtering off irrelevant information?**
- Security support - information sharing brings the problems of security. There will always be a certain amount of information that

cannot be shared and security must be provided to prevent access to this. **Does the product provide facilities for data security?**

- Support for multi-media - multi-media data will play an increasingly important role in the business world and all groupware products will have to exploit it. **Can the product handle all forms of multi-media data such as sound, image and video?**
- Support for standards - as organisations are moving to an open systems approach, it is important that products adhere to the necessary open systems standards. **Does the product adhere to the relevant open systems standards?**

Chapter 6. Introduction to the groupware pyramid principle

The implementation of groupware will require both structural and cultural transformations to take place within an organisation. There will also need to be a technical review of the existing IT infrastructure to determine whether it is suitable and capable of operating under the strain of the groupware products.

There are a number of other issues concerned with ensuring that a groupware solution is successful and we hope to address all of these in the remainder of this book. With the myriad of issues, the potential problems that exist, the enormous change that an organisation and its employees have to go through and the problems of selecting the appropriate groupware products, groupware cannot be implemented in an ad hoc, unplanned fashion. Throwing people into teams and presenting them with groupware products will not achieve anything but distress and potential disaster.

A groupware methodology is required that takes into account all the steps which need to be carried out to ensure:

- a simple and effective transition to the new organisational structure and culture
- that the groupware implementation is successful
- the continuing success of computer supported cooperative team working.

The groupware pyramid principle is such a methodology and identifies three foundations upon which the continuing success of groupware and team working can be built. Once the foundations of the pyramid have been put in place, the groupware solution can be spread right across the organisation until complete corporate buy-in has been achieved. At this stage the company should be operating in a process-oriented, customer-facing structure, with individuals working in cohesive teams built around business processes. The rest of the book is organised around the pyramid principle with chapters reflecting each of the four sections shown below.

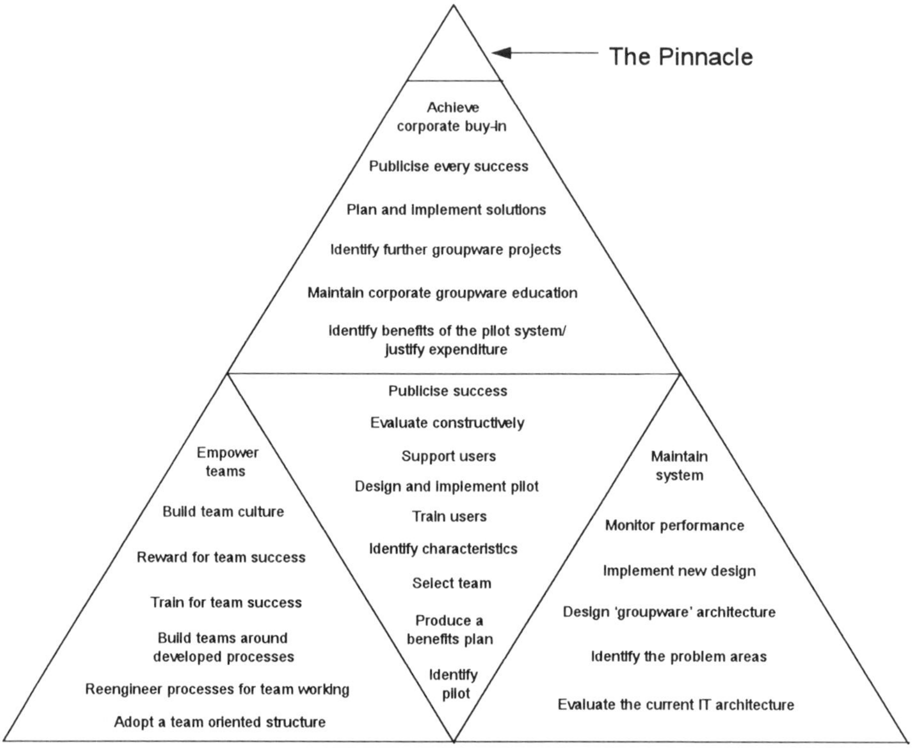

Figure 6.1 The groupware pyramid

The four sections of the pyramid consist of three foundation sections which must be in place before the 'lid' can be put on and the pinnacle reached. Reaching the pinnacle may take a long time, but once there, a company can reap all the many and varied benefits which a groupware solution can bring.

6.1 Moving to groupware

This foundation block involves the transformation that must occur in the structure and culture of the organisation if groupware is to be a success. Groupware can be successful in traditionally organised companies but will be much more successful in organisations which have adopted a team working environment within a network management structure. This section is therefore concerned with making the move to this form of organisation. The main steps in this process are:

- analyse existing culture and structure
- identify business processes and reengineer them for team working
- build work teams around the business processes
- empower the teams and manage the cultural change
- change company procedures in the areas of remuneration and bonus schemes and in the selection of new employees.

6.2 Implementing groupware

The complex nature of a groupware implementation means that it is best to start small and then grow from a solid implementation bed. Groupware needs to be introduced into a company in the form of a pilot project which centres around one or more teams of committed and enthusiastic individuals and achieves instant benefits by approaching obvious problems with the current way of working. The pilot system can be implemented in step with the change in company structure and culture and should help to identify the potential problems that may occur when the groupware implementation is spread out across the organisation. The main steps are thus:

- identify an appropriate pilot project which can achieve 'quick hits' and demonstrable benefits with group(s) of enthusiastic and intelligent individuals who are extremely adaptable
- begin an education programme to emphasise to employees and managers the benefits of groupware and why it is being introduced into the organisation
- implement the pilot project as quickly as possible so that benefits are realised immediately
- publicise the success of the project and begin to identify other areas within the organisation which could obtain significant benefits from groupware.

6.3 Architecture for groupware

For a groupware implementation to be a success, the organisation must have the appropriate IT infrastructure. Without the necessary networking, communication, central data repository, etc., the groupware implementation will not realise all of the potential benefits. Creating the necessary IT architecture can be achieved as the culture and structure is being changed and as the pilot is being introduced. It requires an organisation to:

- evaluate the current IT architecture/infrastructure
- identify the problem areas
- design the new architecture to support groupware
- implement that design and monitor its performance making enhancements where necessary.

6.4 Justifying expense and achieving corporate buy-in

Once the foundations have been put in place, the final building block can be put in place. At this stage, the company should be in a position where it has the necessary structure and culture for groupware to be successful, has already proved the benefits of groupware through a pilot project and has the necessary IT infrastructure to support the proposed groupware solution. Once the benefits of the pilot have been identified, widely reported and publicised, justification for further groupware projects can be provided. This process will continue until corporate buy-in is achieved and the pinnacle is reached.

It is important to note that it is only possible to climb to the pinnacle if all of the foundation blocks are in place.

6.5 The problems of missing foundation blocks

A missing foundation block has the potential to completely destroy the implementation of a groupware system. Ensuring that a firm foundation is in place prior to a large scale implementation can prevent the pyramid from collapsing.

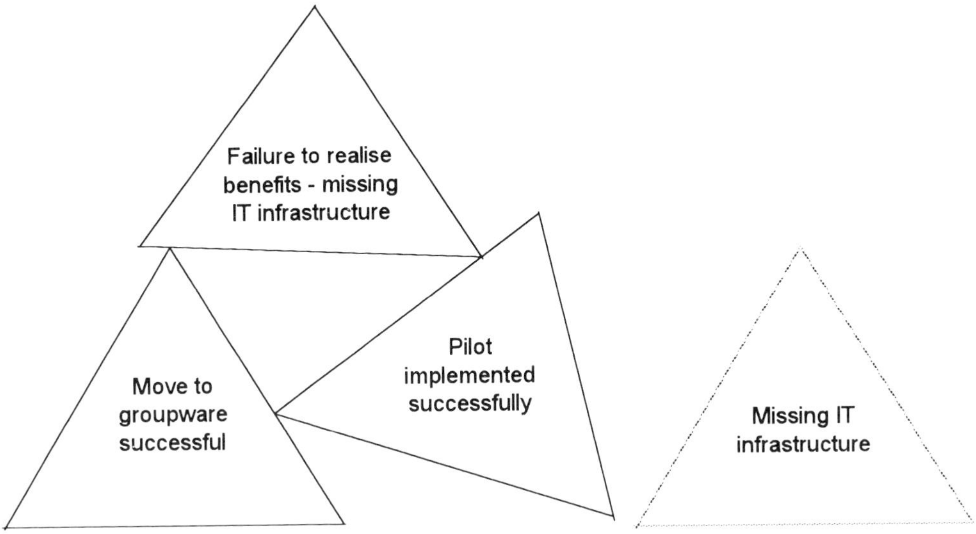

Figure 6.2 A collapsed pyramid

6.5.1 Missing organisational change

The first scenario concerns a UK organisation which was implementing workflow automation software into its claims processing department. It brought in outside consultants to put the necessary IT architecture in place and to run the pilot system with a small set of the work force. The pilot was a great success and increased worker productivity by an impressive amount. Business benefits were identified and a justifiable business case was built for expanding the system to cover the whole claims processing department.

Members of the department were aware of the successes of the pilot and were educated as to the benefits that the groupware solution could bring them. Prior to the implementation, they were organised into work teams based purely on who the management thought would work well together. They were not consulted about the team building exercise and were not involved in the process of deciding who would work together. Education as to the benefits of team working was not given and employees found it a massive culture shock to move from their previously individual way of working. This resulted in the final implementation of the workflow software being a disaster. Team members did not work well together and those members who previously held supervisory roles could not cope with their transition to an ordinary worker. Competition was rife amongst teams and employees continued to work for themselves rather than for the good of the team.

The company realised their mistake and underwent a comprehensive team building exercise. Individual characteristics were assessed and teams were built from those employees whose personalities would complement each other. Workers were also educated about the benefits of team working and attended training courses concentrating on team building skills such as communication, how to give and receive criticism and motivational abilities.

6.5.2 Missing pilot system

The second scenario concerns the implementation of e-mail across the breadth of an organisation. In this case, the company was already organised around work groups, with the entire company structure based around reengineered business processes. The company also had very good IT services and the infrastructure for a company wide e-mail service was immediately available. Over the space of two weeks, e-mail facilities were put on the desktop of each employee without prior warning. No pilot system was carried out, although it may not have been essential in this case, but most importantly no publicity was given about the implementation and no prior training was received.

Over the weeks that followed the implementation, people slowly began to realise that they had this facility and those who knew how to use it began to do so. They soon stopped though as they realised that nobody was reading the messages they were sending. This awful situation ended when the company went back to the drawing board and performed the implementation again. This time they produced the necessary publicity, user benefits management and an initial pilot system which allowed them to judge the training and education needs of their work force.

6.5.3 Inadequate IT infrastructure

In the last scenario, a division of a large UK company was implementing a substantial office automation system which was to provide standardised desktop services to hundreds of users. They had completed the first foundation block remarkably well. Users were involved in the implementation from the start with a user group being established and regular user meetings being conducted. Work groups were identified and regular news sheets publicised the benefits that the new office automation system would bring and how it would change working life for the better. The pilot had been a great success, users were undergoing training to prepare them for the new system and everyone was looking forward to its introduction at the planned implementation date.

The user benefits side of this project was carried out very successfully, but while the users were being convinced of the benefits of the new system and the pilot was proving a great success, the infrastructure which was needed to roll out the full system was not being put in place. The problems with the infrastructure implementation meant that the roll-out date was missed and missed again and missed again. This caused great dissatisfaction to the users who had been looking forward to receiving the new system and had made all the necessary changes in preparation. While they were kept waiting, they started to become disillusioned with the whole process as the roll-out date kept being put back. When they finally received the system, all their enthusiasm had gone and the implementation was viewed as a failure.

6.5.4 Summary

These scenarios highlight the need for a sound foundation before the pyramid's lid can be put in place. If any one of the foundation blocks is missing, it can spell disaster. There are of course exceptions to this but in general, organisational change, a pilot project and the IT architecture must all be dealt with for groupware to be successful. The foundation blocks can and should be put in place in parallel to ensure that all the necessary facilities are available at the same time, allowing the final implementation is carried out without undue delay.

Section III. Moving to groupware

Chapter 7. Creating a groupware environment

Many authors in the field of management studies and business transformation would agree that a new form of organisation will take us into the twenty-first century. This organisation will have strategies, cultures and structures which are remarkably different to those that have served us so well over the past twenty years or more [*Limerick 1991*]. It will offer new opportunities as well as problems to management and will demand new mindsets, skills and competencies from those within it. The predicted success of groupware may be attributable to the fact that it will provide significant help in this transformation.

Jim Manzi of Lotus Development Corporation sums up this change:

> "Organisations are going through massive change. Layers of management are being peeled away, replaced by teams of people assembled on an ad hoc, project or task basis. Teams are created according to the need at hand, then dismantled. Team members are selected based on expertise, not title. Teams are not rooted in any particular location."

Other authors have made similar comments:

> "The organisations that have positioned themselves for success are those that focus on empowering their work forces" [*Wellins 1992*].
>
> "Many companies are using self-managed teams to move from a traditional management structure to a system that gives employees much greater responsibility and involvement" [*Carr 1992*].

The organisations of the future will revolve around what has become known as 'collaborative individualism'. Team working will replace the outmoded, adversarial approach that has grown between management and labour and that now threatens the competitiveness of many organisations throughout the world. Brown and Watts [*Brown and Watts 1992*] believe that the central consequence of this new organisational model is the emergence of an intimately connected human/technology partnership.

The introduction of groupware provides this human/technology partnership and facilitates a team working culture by providing tools which enable individuals to work effectively together.

7.1 The benefits of team working

The reason that many experts are advocating team work and that many organisations have adopted this philosophy is because it has proved to bring substantial benefits. An executive survey conducted by the American Society for Training and Development received responses from 230 Human Resource Development executives about their experience with team working. This survey found that [*Montebello and Buzzotta 1993*]:

- productivity improved in 77 per cent of the respondents' companies
- quality improvements due to team work were reported in 72 per cent of the companies
- waste was reduced in 55 per cent of the firms
- job satisfaction improved in 65 per cent of the respondents' firms
- customer satisfaction improved in 57 per cent.

Additional benefits that were given included more efficient production scheduling, improved production goal setting, and the increased ability of team members to resolve their own disputes.

Clay Carr [*Carr 1992*] also cites many examples where team working has proved to be a great success. He reports quoted productivity gains of between 20 per cent and 50 per cent in organisations which have adopted a team working strategy. Carr also takes time to warn that team working may not always bring the benefits that are expected of it. He points out that moving to a team based structure puts tremendous cultural strain on the organisation and notes that in the recent recessionary times, many firms that had attempted to move to team working have since begun to revert to traditional management techniques.

The success stories from team working far outweigh the ones that ended in disaster. Statistical and case studies also strongly support the idea that team work can achieve enormous success. Tom Peters, the management guru, believes whole heartedly in the team principle and states in his book 'Thriving on Chaos' that:

> "I observe that the power of the team is so great that it is often wise to violate common sense and force a team structure on almost anything".

We do not necessarily agree with this rather rash statement but do agree that team working can realise huge benefits if it is appropriate for the particular organisation and is implemented with careful planning and management. If teams are empowered, i.e., given the tools and responsibility they need to carry out their function without the need for direct supervision, they can achieve even greater success.

It is widely recognised that those organisations that have positioned themselves for future success are those that focus on empowering their work forces. This involves liberating teams of employees and giving them the greater participation, flexibility and autonomy that they have come to desire in recent years. Team work can be more productive, can produce higher quality and is more cost-efficient than solo efforts. Team work also tends to improve job satisfaction, motivation and employee morale.

Although groupware can be successful in traditionally organised companies, it is far less likely to succeed because of the 'individual' culture which is present. Therefore we recommend that prior to a groupware implementation a team working culture is established. This does not necessarily have to be adopted across the breadth of the organisation but can begin with the area in which the pilot groupware system will be implemented. In the sections which follow, we will provide some useful guidelines which can be followed to successfully adopt a team working structure and the associated culture.

It is worth noting here that cultural change is not the only issue which an organisation has to address when planning a groupware implementation. There are several others including:

- business process redesign
- providing education, support and training
- matching the needs of the work groups with the available groupware technology
- creating the necessary IT infrastructure
- selecting an appropriate pilot system and ensuring it is a success.

7.2 Employees' resistance to change

It was once said that "the only constant thing in the world today is change" and this is most definitely true. Change, if it can be shown to be for the better, is welcomed by many people. If the change has some positive consequence on their lives, then people will usually be willing to adapt.

The problem with change in the business environment is that it is inherently difficult to persuade people that the change they are undergoing is for the better. This may be due to the fact that change in an organisation is usually dramatic, requiring the individual to work under a whole new regime, in a different management structure, with different colleagues and using a different set of tools. When the change being made involves a number of factors, it is a lot more difficult to convince people that their new way of working will be beneficial to them.

Humans naturally resist change because alterations in our lifestyle upset our status quo. Even if we know that the change is going to benefit us, there is never any guarantee of this and the fear of the unknown is always present. Lanny Blake [*Blake 1992*] illustrated this resistance by describing what may have happened the first time that man tried to change, influence, convince, control or otherwise transform his community. We will now share some of his ideas with you.

7.2.1 Man's first change

The first time that man tried to change his community or environment in some way could have happened over 20 million years ago when an innovative tribe leader tried to convince his group to move from their shelter under a tree into a nearby cave to escape from the rain, cold winds and potential predators.

This move was obviously for the tribe's own good but still they resisted the relocation. For them, the tree was more than adequate and had been their home for some time - they knew the tree and felt safe there. It kept off most of the rain, provided some shade when necessary and they only had to contend with a few carnivorous creatures. They admitted that the bird population was a problem and that the insects did tend to bite rather a lot but they thought that the number of tribe members dying from exposure was reassuringly small.

After hearing all of the reasons why the tribe shouldn't move, the leader listed the reasons why they should. He told them that the cave would stop all the rain, would provide some extra warmth, would keep out all of the predators and would rid them of the target-practising bird population. He also emphasised that they could always visit their old homestead whenever they pleased because it was only fifty yards away from the cave opening.

On hearing the speech given by their leader, the tribe were curious as to how he knew so much. He told them that he had visited the cave and upon this was reminded that one visit isn't a lifetime or a guarantee that changing will improve the tribe's quality of life or make the community safer. The leader responded by telling them stories that had been passed down from the elders. These tales described how the tribe had previously lived on the plains and had made the migration to the shelter of the tree when under the influence of a very powerful leader. He emphasised the fact that those members that had refused to move were soon eaten by predators or killed by the harsh weather.

The tribe understand the leader's objectives better now and agree to undertake a study of the benefits that could be obtained from the move. The leader must provide a detailed plan of how the move will take place and if the plan is not successful, the leader will be executed!

We are sure that on reading this passage, many of the concepts contained therein will be familiar to you and be ones that you have experienced in the past. Persuading people that change is for the best is extremely difficult and those people suggesting the change, ultimately gain the responsibility for ensuring that it is a success. The same people have to bear the rather harsh consequences if it fails.

The reasons given to the tribe for the move were perfectly valid and made absolute sense - there were no drawbacks. The tribe had moved before and had benefited from this, so why can't they move again? Blake says that many managers would agree that the same question can be asked of today's employees when it comes to making changes. He goes on to say that:

> "generating receptivity to change requires that organisation members understand the pressures, both external and internal, that make the change necessary".

Moving to a team based structure, with employees having to communicate, cooperate, collaborate and share their information with each other, will require a huge shift in culture. Employees will have to accept a totally new way of working and will have to understand the concepts of cooperating to achieve success. The story given above highlights that employees will resist such changes unless they are implemented very carefully with employee participation from the very outset. It is essential to remember that: 'people are better led than driven'.

7.3 Building successful work teams

> "We can say without hesitation that almost every single good thing that has happened within this company over the past few years can be traced back to the liberation of some individual, some team or some business unit" [*John Welsh* in *Thompson and Strickland 1990*].

Building teams based around work processes can enable you to liberate your work force; to 'empower' them. This requires fewer layers of management and helps in the process of moving to a network management structure. By driving down responsibility to the work group, employees can be given control of their day-to-day activities without the need for direct supervision. This will increase worker productivity and boost employee morale amongst other things.

Basing teams around work processes also has many benefits. Most organisations currently operate in the situation where they have conceptualised functions, fragmented tasks and sequential, simplified activities that reflect the assembly-line style of design. As we move through the 1990s and into the next century, it is becoming increasingly apparent that work processes are becoming a lot more complex. They are no longer linear and therefore cannot be simplified into strings of quick, sequential tasks. When a task that produces an end result in simplified and fragmented, it effectively robs the people who perform the task of any self-esteem, sense of accomplishment or pride in their work.

The productivity and quality that companies demand requires a high degree of collaboration among people, departments and functions in order to complete these processes. It has been found that companies with the highest sustained productivity growth focus less on how their individual departments perform and more on how the departments work together as products move between them. Many organisations are discovering what the Japanese learned long ago: that people, along with technology and marketing ploys, are a vital resource and a means of improving productivity.

The steps involved in moving to a team based structure can be identified as follows:

- identify business processes to which teams can be attached
- design and build successful teams around these processes
- train the teams in the use of the new tools and procedures and introduce them to the team working philosophy
- review the assessment and reward procedures within the company
- review the selection procedure for prospective employees.

7.3.1 Identifying business processes

Organisational change is one of the major business imperatives of the 1990s and companies are beginning to realise that their business processes or work places need to be redesigned if they are to remain competitive. The move to a team working environment and the introduction of groupware can and should be the initiator of this reorchestration.

It also provides the organisation with the opportunity to move to a process oriented structure where teams are organised around business processes as opposed to functional units. This means that the company is organised so that its strategy and central functions, such as corporate finance and human resources, are shared between business units which service product groups.

Business process reengineering can be seen as a process that achieves radical learning and change in work processes and employee skills through clean slate 'breakthrough' projects [*Brown and Watts 1992*]. The key word in this description is breakthrough. In reengineering processes, companies should strive to achieve a breakthrough and revolutionise the way that the processes are carried out. By achieving this radical new way of working, teams are forced to think about the processes they are carrying out and a high degree of learning takes place. There are two fundamental tasks in creating this breakthrough:

- thoroughly analysing the root causes of customer satisfaction problems and 'waste' in existing workflow processes
- using this analysis to create the ideal value stream to deliver value with far less work.

Once these tasks have been carried out, the processes can be reengineered by carrying out the three steps identified by CSC Index:

- Redesign - the business processes are completely revamped to achieve new standards and productivity increases.
- Retooling - using appropriate groupware tools to build applications and the correct human/technology partnership to enable the process to be carried out.
- Reorchestration - educating and supporting the team in the transition to the new processes and technology environment.

During the redesign phase of the process, it is worthwhile considering the characteristics of a job which make them appealing to employees and teams. There are five characteristics which are inherent in any job [*Montebello and Buzzotta 1993*]:

- Skill Variety - various job activities which call for different skills and talents. The more skills and talents that are involved in a job, the more interesting it will be to the people performing the function.

- Task Identity - the extent to which a job is handled from beginning to end, producing an identifiable and complete outcome which can give a sense of satisfaction and accomplishment. The higher the sense of achievement that is felt once the task is complete, the more enjoyable it will be.
- Task Significance - the extent to which the work has an effect on others or on society in general. The more significant the task, the greater the responsibility that will be felt by the team completing the task to finish it successfully.
- Autonomy - the freedom and discretion in planning, organising, scheduling and performing the work. Sense of achievement and responsibility will increase with the autonomy given to workers. It has also recently become apparent that workers hold the key to making changes in work processes that can have dramatic impacts on productivity. Giving the team autonomy will allow them to make small incremental changes to the way that they work every day in order to complete the process in the most efficient way possible.
- Feedback - clear and direct information about performance and effectiveness. Employees want to be rewarded for their efforts in monetary terms but also in positive feedback about their progress or standard of work. If during the completion of a process, they get immediate feedback about the quality of that work, this will keep them motivated. Hopefully they will have a sense of pride about their work and a drop in standards will spur them in to increasing their efforts.

Research has shown that jobs with high degrees of these five characteristics tend to motivate workers with the result being a significant impact on business performance. Team work designed with these five characteristics can help to organise simplified tasks into a unit that focuses on an important business objective such as quality or customer service.

Teams completing tasks in which the characteristics are present are challenged by worthwhile and important job results as opposed to performing simple activities that are carefully monitored by a supervisor. Workers have autonomy over their work and the ability to design their own work procedures which best suit them and their team;

they are not bound to strict and prescriptive rules. They are able to determine, on a regular basis, whether their performance is satisfactory and are motivated enough and have the autonomy to take positive action if this falls below their expected level. There are two guidelines or principles which can be followed in an attempt to define processes possessing the five characteristics:

- Combining tasks - when defining the tasks to be carried out by a team, it is better to take several existing smaller tasks and combine these into one larger module. This larger module can then be given to a team who have the autonomy to see it through from start to finish.
- Establishing client relationships - how many times have you heard a statement such as: 'the employees had no sense of how their jobs contributed to the final solution for the customer'. When this is the case, employees can gain little satisfaction from their work because they have no idea about the contribution it is making to the organisation. This is especially true if they perform work in the middle of a process and therefore do not see the beginning or end of the work cycle. Teams who have the opportunity to deal directly with the people who use their work - whether these be internal or external customers - see immediate increases in skill variety, autonomy and feedback. It is recognised that when companies empower teams to accomplish a meaningful business result (better customer service), workers gain greater influence over the work processes and are motivated to contribute to organisational goals.

7.3.2 Building successful teams

Organising your work force into teams is not an easy exercise. There are so many aspects and issues which need to be considered when initiating a team building process that planning the change is essential. The issues that need to be addressed include:

- some employees will be more adaptable to the change than others
- some employees will be better 'team players' than others
- reengineering processes carried out by workers will mean pointing out their imperfections - some workers will not be receptive to this confrontation

- working in a team requires people to share their information and skills
- some employees may not be willing to share their knowledge
- working in a team requires a whole new set of interpersonal skills.

When building work teams, there are five points which must be considered prior to their implementation [*Carr 1992*]:

No universally applicable technology

There is no universally applicable technology of work organisation and management. Many new techniques and technologies emerge as being the cure-all of all business problems and groupware is no exception to this. No one technique can be because a business consists of three structures and a new technique never covers all the aspects. A business will have a mission, technology and culture. Groupware provides advances in technology to meet the mission but without changes in the culture to take advantage of groupware, it will not be successful. Teams should therefore be created as logical extensions of existing values wherever possible to minimise the effects of cultural change.

Provide clear goals

'Our goal is to implement teams' is an inadequate goal and will almost certainly fail. When teams are not implemented as a reaction to a clear business need, they will at best be a distraction and a waste. 'We are creating teams to take advantage of groupware' is also not a valid reason for implementing teams. The reason must be a response to a clear business requirement which may be the driver for the groupware implementation which in turn becomes the driver for teams.

Teams succeed when they have clear, worthwhile and compelling goals and team members know that they are expected to commit themselves to these goals. Clear, worthwhile and compelling are all very important words. The goals must be clear and also be achievable, they must be specific and to the point - 'our aim is to increase productivity' is not adequate but 'our aim is to reduce customer complaints by 20 per cent over the next six months with regard to product range X' is a clear aim. The goals must be worthwhile for the team who are trying to achieve them and they must commit themselves to them.

Reward for team success

Teams succeed when members are rewarded for team success, not just on individual merit. Most organisations still reward employees for individual performance and people still get ahead by proving that they are the best, perhaps by showing up a colleague's inadequacies in the process. To enable teams to operate successfully, rewards must be given for team success. This point is discussed further in a following section.

The role of middle managers

Traditionally, when moving to a team based structure, firms see no place within their organisation for their existing first and second level management; this is a mistake. The emergence of self-managed and empowered teams removes the need for the layers of middle management found in traditionally organised companies. These members of staff represent a significant reservoir of knowledge and experience which cannot be disregarded merely because their roles have become unnecessary. Moving to a team based structure can be a lengthy process and the experience of the middle management can be invaluable in this transition. Many organisations simply make the managers ordinary team members but this is unsatisfactory both for the managers involved and for the members of the team that used to operate under their control. Instead, the managers should be allowed to grow and develop with the teams, perhaps taking on the role of the coach, consultant or mediator and using their knowledge to resolve the problems which will undoubtedly arise in the initial stages of team working. They could also take on any of the following responsibilities:

- coaching and training the team members
- serving as the contact points for suppliers
- helping teams gain access to the resources and training that are needed
- filling in when team members are absent or during peak demand periods
- helping teams to coordinate their efforts with other teams and other units within the organisation.

If approached intelligently, a firm should find that it has to forcibly reassign or dismiss few, if any, supervisors. It is the firm's responsibility to help their middle managers make a successful transition. If this is ignored the company may find itself losing a wealth of knowledge and experience unnecessarily.

Potential conflicts must be anticipated

Teams that are significantly self-managing will create conflict with the existing culture. This conflict must be anticipated, planned for and successfully resolved - or else. We have already talked extensively about the change in culture which comes with the transition to team working. Empowering teams does conflict with traditionally organised companies which operate through hierarchically structured power and dependence. This conflict must be anticipated and planned for so that the strain put on the employees involved is not too great.

7.3.3 Empowering teams

Empowering teams is essential if they are to realise the benefits expected of them. Giving teams and their members the knowledge, information, resources, responsibility and authority that they need to carry out their tasks will give them the autonomy that they need to be motivated and obtain satisfaction from their work. Moving responsibility down the levels of hierarchy to the bottom level worker also removes the need for layers of middle management. This enables a firm to operate in a flatter and more responsive organisational structure. The process of driving responsibility down to the team level is sometimes known as vertical loading. With vertical loading, responsibilities and controls that were formally reserved for high-level managers are added to a team's job.

This addition utilises the brain power and skills of the team more effectively and generally results in some form of productivity or efficiency improvement. There are a number of tasks which can be transferred from supervisory roles to the work group and these include [*Montebello and Buzzotta 1993*]:

- assigning work activities on a daily basis
- changing the processes involved in a task
- performing appraisals for colleagues in the team
- project planning and management

- responsibility for quality management
- self development in the form of training
- determining the remuneration and rewards of team members
- preparing progress reports and presentations
- managing the budget
- sales and marketing activities.

Others important points to note when in the process of building teams are [*Blake 1992*]:

- an anxious group member inhibits group functioning
- people with special skills relative to the group task will have more influence on group decisions
- participation in group tasks decreases with increases in group size - small is better
- the probability of a leader emerging increases with group size
- participants usually rate small groups as more satisfactory, positive and effective than large groups
- the probability of group conformity to a unanimous majority increases with increasing group size
- the probability of social participation increases with the age of group members.

Chapter 8. Developing the team culture

Once the work force has been organised into teams built around reengineered business processes, the team culture must be fully developed. This involves monitoring the progress of the teams, training team members in the art of effective team working, changing the reward structure to encourage collaboration and reviewing the selection procedure for prospective employees.

8.1 Modelling the growth of the team

There are a number of models which have been developed to explain the stages that a team must go through before it can become truly effective. All emphasise the need for team members to learn to work together and to realise that cooperation, communication and information sharing are vital to team success. Trust and reliability are also important factors in achieving team success and are properties which must be instilled when teams are established.

Most of the models mentioned above define a similar progression within the team from a stage where team members are assessing each other's capabilities and getting used to sharing information and cooperating, to the stage where they are involved in truly collaborative teamwork. In making this progression, the team will go through many stressful periods and trial and error will play an important role in enabling them to discover the best way to work cohesively. If the team is empowered, they will also redefine the way they complete tasks a number of times to bring out the best in each member. The four main stages in this progression are explained below:

8.1.1 Stage 1 - Cautious affiliation

This is mainly an exploration stage where team members are getting used to working together and are effectively 'establishing their territory'. Little is accomplished during this stage - productivity is low as the team comes to grips with the new way of working. The main points to note in this stage are:

- team members are likely to be anxious about what the team and they, as individual members, are supposed to do
- team members will be concerned about their personal ability to complete the necessary tasks and also the combined ability of the team
- team members will assess each other's abilities and attitudes and try to gauge where each person will fit into the group
- if the team is empowered, work procedures will be changed frequently to suit particular members' style of working.
- working relationships remain cautious and noncommittal.

8.1.2 Stage 2 - Competitiveness

This is the stage where team members begin to accept that team working requires a totally different culture. They start to realise that team working is more difficult than they had initially imagined. Points to note are:

- the gap between their expectations of team working and the reality that they are facing will cause frustration among team members
- there will be a lot of blaming, defensiveness, destructive disagreement and test confrontation as problems start to emerge
- this will be a real test of character for team members and it will be at this stage that certain members will begin to dominate. The now redundant middle managers will be invaluable in this stage and can use their managerial experience to overcome the 'people problems'
- subgroups may start to form around conflicting beliefs. This must be resolved and again managerial skills are essential
- questions of team goals, missions, tasks and roles will begin to arise

- finding answers to these questions will help to build bonds between members and slowly the team will move towards its objectives and work more cohesively.

8.1.3 Stage 3 - Harmonious cohesiveness

In this stage, team members begin to work together with great effect. All animosity towards those who have adopted 'leadership' roles is lost and members of the team support each other in working towards common goals and aims. Interpersonal patterns develop within the group as members learn how to get the best out of each other.

- competitive relationships become cooperative
- communication channels open and feelings of mutual trust deepen
- members begin to get the feeling of 'groupness' and become proud to be associated with the team.

8.1.4 Stage 4 - Collaborative teamwork

This is the stage where the group of individuals becomes a truly collaborative team.

- structured processes and procedures emerge to allocate resources, resolve personal conflicts, deal with the larger organisation, give warranted positive feedback and discipline members for unacceptable behaviour
- the team begins to make decisions about task and process, diagnosing and solving problems and choosing and implementing actions and changes
- members freely share and pool viewpoints and information to make sound decisions.

An alternative behavioural model, developed by Psychological Associates, identifies two common categories of behaviour which are commonly exhibited by teams:

- getting things done - teams set direction, plan, organise and structure their activities to get things done
- building strong relationships - teams work to build strong relationships by fostering open communication and by getting

involvement and commitment whether they are making decisions, conducting meetings or resolving conflicts.

Figure 8.1 describes the characteristics of each of the four stages in an alternative way: Forming, Storming, Norming and Performing. These models are important because they allow for potential problems to be identified and anticipated so that when they occur - and they almost always will - they can be dealt with swiftly.

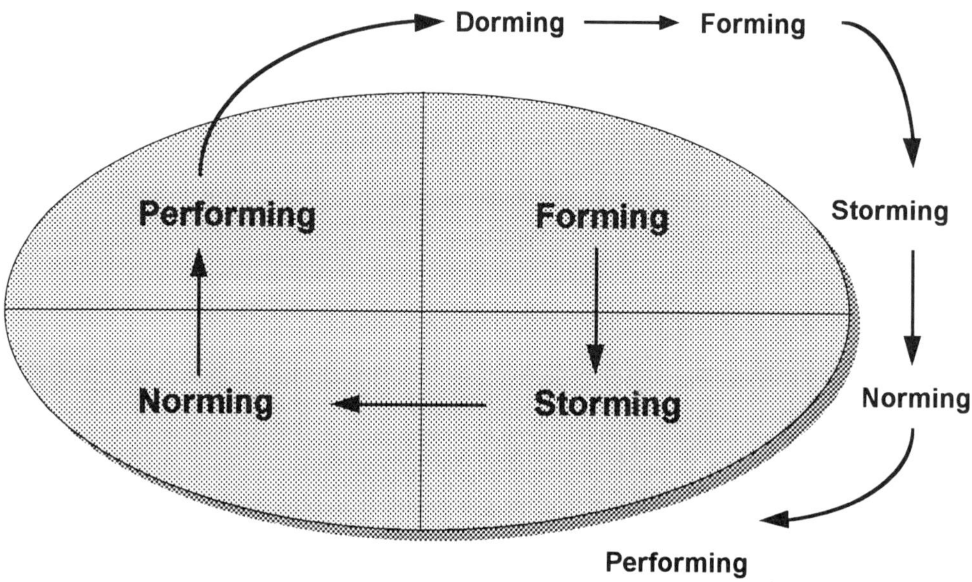

Figure 8.1a The four stages of team development

It is important to note that team building does not happen and then just end dramatically once the team has made it to stage 3 or 4. Team building is a on-going activity. The team must continually strive for greater success and must put in place stringent standards against which they can appraise their work.

This diagnosis process must highlight the inefficiencies and enable them to redefine their work activities to eliminate these. Teams must also maintain their level of knowledge by establishing training and development programmes which will also build upon their strengths and rid them of their weaknesses.

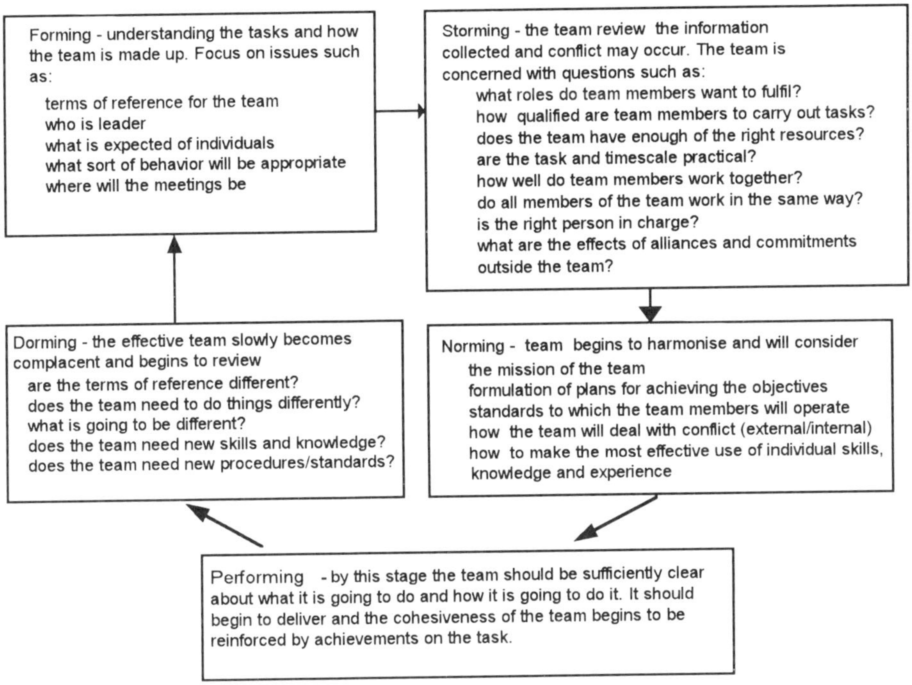

Figure 8.1b The four stages of team development

8.2 Training teams for success

Moving to a team-oriented environment requires team members to acquire a whole new set of skills, especially interpersonal ones. Many organisations underestimate the need for training to help employees gain such skills. Working in teams usually involves multi-skilling and job rotation and the members of successful teams generally spend 20 per cent of their time during the first year involved in training activities. There are three categories of training which are essential for team success [*Wellins 1992*]:

- job skills - the technical skills to allow the person to perform their function and be involved in job rotation exercises
- team/interaction skills - perhaps the most important training of all, these are the interpersonal and communication skills which are needed to allow cohesive team performance. These skills will probably involve discussion and meeting skills, techniques for

giving and receiving feedback, advice on how to handle conflict and trust building exercises

- quality/action skills - these skills help team members in the process of performing continual analysis of their performance and making changes to improve this. Skills will also be needed to set up quality management guidelines and the procedures for ensuring that these are followed.

Training tends to work better when it is given over time rather than in one lump. This allows team members to build relationships in between the training sessions and therefore make more productive use of the training time. This point would also suggest that interpersonal training is given towards the end when workers have had time to assess each other and realise the need for interpersonal skills and the ability to communicate effectively.

8.3 Modifying the reward structure

Most organisations currently base their reward and remuneration structure around individual performance. When in a team based structure, rewarding for personal achievement creates competition between team members which prevents the team from functioning efficiently. As long as there are incentives for competition within an organisation, people will only aim to further their individual goals to the detriment of the team.

Reward structures must therefore be based around team performance so that members are encouraged to work for the good of the team and equate their personal success with that of the team. Team bonuses could be shared equally among team members or the team members could decide how to distribute the bonus amongst themselves. Many managers could not possibly imagine the latter suggestion being implemented successfully; team members deciding how to divide the bonus amongst themselves. Until this is possible in some form, teams will not operate at their full potential.

8.4 Reviewing the selection procedure

Adopting a team-oriented structure requires that the company's selection procedures be changed to ensure that new employees will fit into the new culture. This means changing the set of competencies that are expected of candidates and even changing the whole selection procedure with new forms of interview and testing. It may be an opportunity to involve existing team members by allowing them to design evaluation techniques and perform the interviews themselves.

When designing the new selection procedure, it is useful to conduct a job analysis. This involves drawing up a list of behaviours, technical knowledge, skills and motivational areas that differentiate successful performers from unsuccessful ones. The knowledge and experience gained from the transition to the team structure can be invaluable in this process. Common dimensions that are looked for in team players are:

- previous experience of team working
- communication skills
- problem identification and solution skills
- learning ability
- use of initiative
- ability to conform to work standards
- coaching and training skills
- motivational ability
- technical knowledge.

Once the dimensions that a successful candidate must possess have been identified, the interview and assessment procedures can be redefined with these in mind. The best selection systems tend to include a combination of techniques including interview, paper-and-pencil cognitive-ability tests, technical tests, reference checks and realistic job previews. The most interesting of these is the 'realistic job preview'. By showing candidates exactly what is involved in their role within the team, those who feel that they cannot adapt to a team working environment will be actively discouraged from accepting any offer of employment.

8.5 Problems of team building

In the real world, not many teams make it to stage four where they act as a cohesive unit working together for the good of the team with no desire to achieve personal success. Those teams that have made it, have worked as a team for a long periods of time and have undergone many personal battles, disagreement, heartache and stress along the way.

Perhaps the main reason that teams hardly ever make it to stage four is competition. Competition is inherent in every worker because humans are naturally ambitious and always want to do better. This competitive nature prevents the team from working for itself as a generic unit - members will always have the ultimate goal of individual success whatever the reward or pay structure of the company.

Other problems that may occur during the team building process are listed below.

8.5.1 Building teams of higher level management

The higher up that you move in an organisation, the more resistance you will encounter to collaborative working. The monetary incentives present in the majority of organisations for upper management act as a disincentive for them to share ideas and information. Their personal information is their powerbase. As long as competitive incentives exist in an organisation, true team working can never be achieved. This may explain the greater success that is achieved when implementing teams at the lower levels of a company. Lower echelon employees are usually used to work group projects and naturally rely heavily on each other, they have fewer incentives to compete and they welcome the chance to be able to air their ideas and share their knowledge base.

8.5.2 Knowledge is power

As George Orwell noted in '1984', "knowledge is power - but there will have to be a mental revolution if people are to surrender this personal power to the company".

We live in a culture where information is equated with power and security and people at all levels within a company will jealously guard islands of vital information. Once this information is made freely available, some people will begin to feel very dispensable. It will therefore require some careful management and assurance of job security if all the information is to be prised out of the work force. This is particularly true of middle and more senior management who may feel that empowering teams makes their job redundant.

It is worth noting that there have been successful groupware projects that have been withdrawn by senior management who began to get worried about the way in which power, access to information and freedom of action was moving swiftly downwards in the organisation.

8.5.3 Selecting team members

When teams are being formed, it is important to group the people who can work well together. If you merely throw people in at the deep end and tell them that they will be working together, you will hardly ever achieve success. Instead, it may be worth interviewing prospective team members to discover who they think they can work with or by issuing personality tests so that a team can be made up from people who are likely to work well together. It is worth bearing in mind that [*Johnsen-Lenz 1992*]:

> "Teams work best in an atmosphere of trust where each person is comfortable expressing themselves openly and listening to others with respect. Team intelligence and creativity is greatest when each member brings all their knowledge to the meeting table".

8.5.4 Isolation

Groupware allows teams to be built independently of where the team members are located. This may lead to certain people being isolated in some remote part of the country or even in a different country in a different time zone. Those isolated from the rest of the team cannot be forgotten about and sometimes electronic communications are not enough. An organisation must consider the environment that remote workers operate in and make sure that procedures are in place to control the stress which may result from the isolation. This point is becoming increasingly apparent as teleworking is becoming more popular.

8.6 Teleworking

Teleworking - working from home or at a location outside of the office - is catching on in popularity according to a recent Gallup survey commissioned by BT. The survey concluded that by 1995, 2.3 million people will be working from home for three or more days a week. There is even a National Association of Teleworking which has recently launched a management certification scheme which aims to bring the benefits of accreditation to teleworkers.

Teleworking has been made a realistic possibility by advances in computer and communications technology which now supports group interactions any time, any place. This means that employees can perform their business function at a remote location, usually at home. Office space is saved, workers become more productive, access to a wider skill base is obtained and Gallup discovered that the benefits shown in Figures 8.2a and 8.2b may occur in many organisations:

The down side to teleworking is the isolation which may be experienced by those working from home. Existing teleworkers that have been interviewed have expressed the following concerns:

- they feel that they are never out of the office
- they end up working longer hours to get things done
- they find it hard to distinguish between work and family
- they feel isolated and when things go wrong or they are having problems.

Even with these disadvantages, teleworking remains a very attractive proposition to many organisations who spend large sums of money housing employees who could perform their function equally as well from home. The growth of teleworking will only be hindered by organisations that do not consider the option; only 39 per cent of the workers canvassed in the Gallup survey would be brave enough to ask permission to work from home. Working from home must not be seen as an easy option.

Once teleworking has become widespread, organisations may even be employing people located in foreign countries!

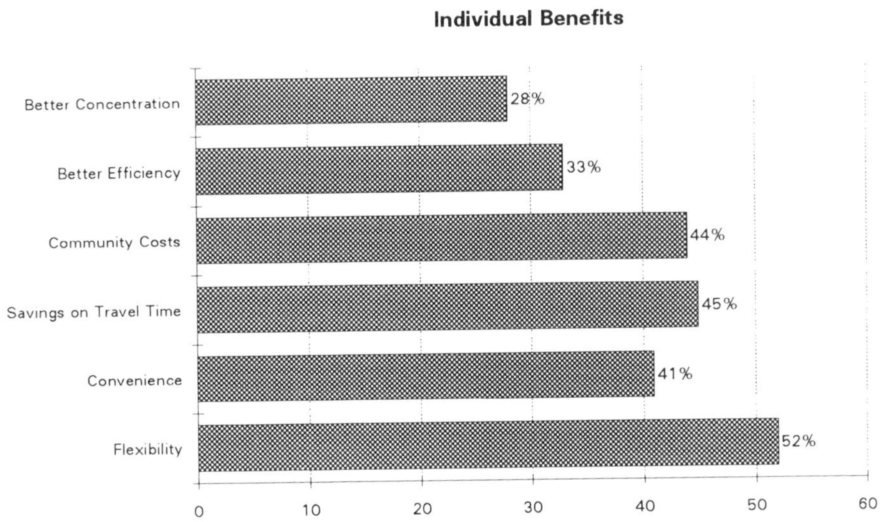

Figure 8.2a The individual benefits of teleworking

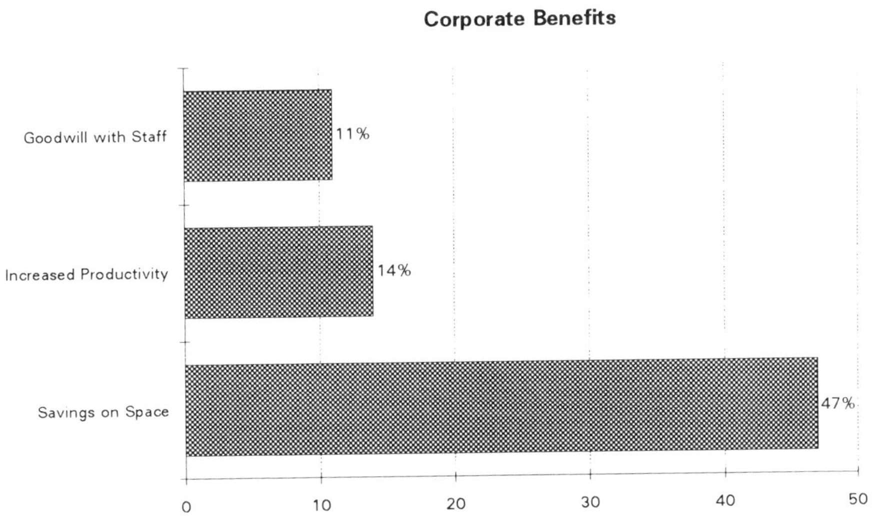

Figure 8.2b The corporate benefits of teleworking

Chapter 9. Creating the human/technology partnership

Brown and Watts [*1992*] believe that the central consequence of the new organisational model which is rapidly evolving is the emergence of an intimately connected human/technology partnership. Groupware can form this partnership by providing tools which proactively support individuals in their desire to work effectively as a team. With so many groupware products and technologies in the market place, selecting the appropriate products is becoming increasingly difficult.

Part of the problem stems from the fact that the needs of individuals and teams will vary significantly across the organisation. The result of this is that any one groupware product is not suitable for everybody. This is an extremely important point and those people responsible for recommending the groupware products to be implemented, must realise that a groupware solution will require the input of a family of products. This will enable each team, and individual within that team, to be given access to the tools which most suit their way of working and assist in achieving their objectives. It cannot be stressed enough that groupware is a family of products and its whole is greater than the sum of its parts.

To help in the selection process, we recommend that a thorough evaluation of each work group is conducted. This will include analysing the characteristics of the work group and also the process that they carry out. This analysis will enable the appropriate products to be chosen, i.e., the ones that best suit the team's way of working.

The model presented by Johansen and described earlier provides a very simple analysis tool. It allows you to identify which groupware technologies are appropriate depending on the location and time of communication between members of the work group. This model is far too simplistic and does not even begin to take into account the characteristics of the particular work group or indeed the processes that they are involved in. There are so many dimensions involved in the analysis of a work group and the associated processes that a framework needs to be developed to allow this to take place.

Mark Roberts of PA Consulting Group began work on such a framework. We have taken this initial work and extended it to allow a thorough evaluation of the work group and processes to be carried out with the result of this analysis helping in the process of choosing the appropriate groupware technology. We believe that once the characteristics of the team and processes have been identified, these can be matched on to the groupware technology which will offer the most appropriate support.

9.1 Analysing the characteristics of the work group

The characteristics of work groups and the technology required to support them will vary considerably across an organisation. Therefore these characteristics must be analysed and identified so that the appropriate groupware technology can be chosen for each team or group of teams. It is likely that there will be a number of teams in an organisation and a thorough evaluation of each would be impractical. In this situation, groups of teams with similar abilities, objectives and work processes should be identified so that the analysis can be carried out at a higher level.

The analysis of the teams can be performed by answering a number of questions relating to the ability of the team, the characteristics of the members and the nature of the tasks that they perform. By answering questions on these topics, a picture of the team can be built up and the groupware technology most appropriate chosen. Out of the groupware technologies identified in Chapter 5, each has benefits and is most suitable to particular work group scenarios. For example, workflow management technology is suited to teams which have little autonomy over their work and follow defined rules and procedures. It is also useful when information always follows a predefined path through the team. On the other hand e-mail facilities are useful when team members have a large degree of autonomy and make decisions about how information flows both internally and externally to the team. A more detailed description of the groupware technologies and which characteristics they are appropriate for is given later in this section.

9.2 Questions to assess work group characteristics

The questions which must be answered in order to identify the characteristics of a work group or larger entity concentrate on four areas:

- Attributes of the work group - these questions concentrate on analysing the interaction between team members and the 'individual' aspects of the team.
- Analysis of the work group activities - these questions provide details of the types of activities performed in the work group.
- Properties of the information being processed - these questions help to identify the information needs of the work group.
- Business issues - these questions relate to general business issues and how they may affect the technology that is chosen.

The following questions should answered on a scale of 1 to 5 so that the differences between teams can be highlighted. The questions should be answered for each work team or larger entity in the organisation.

9.2.1 Attributes of the work group

1. Does the team operate as a cohesive unit? (Cohesiveness)

   Act as individuals (1) .... (5) Cohesive unit

2. How adaptable are team members to change? (Adaptability)

   Do not welcome change (1) .... (5) Welcome change

3. How 'intelligent' or IT literate are member of the team? (Intelligence)

   No IT awareness (1) .... (5) IT literate

4. To what extent do team members share their information? (Sharing)

   No information sharing (1) .... (5) Total information sharing

5. Are team members located locally or spread across diverse locations? (Location)

   Located in same office (1) .... (5) Spread over diverse locations

The questions in this section largely relate to the 'groupness' of the team. The **cohesiveness** of the team will determine whether a product is chosen that makes people work together closely or whether the product should require little collaboration from team members. The **adaptability** and **intelligence** of the group will affect whether the product is complex, requiring radical changes in working practices and culture or not. The amount of information **sharing** that a product requires will be determined by the sharing factor and the functionality that is provided to allow remote team members to communicate will be affected by the **location** aspect.

9.2.2 Analysis of work group activities

1. Do the processes carried out by the work group require much thought? (Thought)

   Easy, repetitive tasks (1) .... (5) Complex tasks

2. How much autonomy do the team members have? (Autonomy)

   Conform to prescriptive rules (1) .... (5) Adapt working environment

3. To what extent are team members required to interact with their colleagues? (Interaction)

   Can work in isolation (1) .... (5) Must interact to complete task

4. Do work group activities vary from day-to-day or are they stable? (Variability)

   Same daily activities (1) .... (5) Unpredictable daily tasks

The **thought** aspect will decide whether the chosen product helps in the completion of complex processes or whether it provides standard services. The **autonomy** of the group and the **variability** of the work will determine how flexible the product should be. The **interaction** factor will decide the degree of communication facilities offered by the product.

9.2.3 Properties of the information being processed

1. Does information arrive from a number of sources? (Sources)

   Sole source (1) .... (5) Wide range of sources

2. Is the information of a variety of types? (Types)

   Same type (1) .... (5) Complex range of data types

3. Is the information being handled of a private or confidential nature? (Confidentiality)

   Public information (1) .... (5) Strictly confidential information

4. Are vast quantities of information processed by the work group? (Quantity)

   Small amount (1) .... (5) Large amount

5. Is the information held for long periods of time? (Time)

   Held for hours (1) .... (5) Held for months/years

6. Is there a recognised path for the flow of information amongst the work group? (Flow)

   Rigid information flows (1) .... (5) Information takes varying paths

The factors of **sources**, **types**, **quantity** and **time** will be reflected in the information handling abilities of the product - the greater the degree of each of these, the more sophisticated the information handling abilities of the chosen product. The security features offered by the selected software will be affected by the **confidentiality** of the data being processed and the rigidity of the information **flow** will determine how prescriptive the product makes the flow of information throughout the work group.

9.2.4 Business issues

1. Is the process being carried out critical to business success? (Criticality)

   Internal, non-critical process (1) .... (5) Critical to business success

2. Will the activities of the work group evolve? (Evolution)

   Static processes (1) .... (5) Continually evolving area

3. Are management committed to the introduction/development of work group computing? (Commitment)

   Reluctant to change and invest (1) .... (5) Strongly committed to change

4. How knowledgeable are the work force to the benefits of groupware? (Knowledge)

   No knowledge of concepts (1) .... (5) Fully understand the benefits

The complexity and reliability of the product will be determined by the **criticality** of the processes being carried out in the work group. The flexibility of the chosen product with regard to scaleability and ease of development will be controlled by the **evolution** of the business processes. The **commitment** of managers and the **knowledge** of work force will affect the radicality of the product and whether it should be chosen for short term benefits (quick hits) or long term strategic aims.

9.2.5 Analysing the questionnaire results

Answering the above questions will not lead you straight to the ideal groupware product or set of products but it will help you to gauge the types or categories of technology that are required. Even if it does not achieve this aim, it will make you think about the issues involved when deciding on the appropriate groupware product and the system that is to be developed using it.

The rating system of the questions is meant to be ad hoc and 'comparative' rather than exact. If the analysis is performed on a number of work groups, the rating system can be used to judge the differences in the characteristics of the work groups and the processes that they are involved in. This comparison may help to identify fundamental difference that make different groupware technologies appropriate for each work group.

Once the questions have been answered, the results can be used to draw up a picture of the work group and to subsequently match this against the groupware technologies. This picture is best visualised in the form of a spider diagram. The following example shows the results of the analysis performed on a work group involved in the processing of customer applications for mortgages.

9.2.6 Example analysis

This analysis was performed on a work group involved in processing mortgage applications. The building society involved offered a whole portfolio of different mortgages. This particular team were responsible for overseeing the applications for a particular mortgage offering from the stage of receiving the application to the stage of acceptance or rejection.

Attributes of the work group	**Analysis of work group activities**
• cohesiveness - 4 • adaptability - 3 • intelligence - 3 • sharing - 4 • location - 1	• thought - 2 • autonomy - 2 • interaction - 3 • variability - 1
Properties of the information • sources - 1 • types - 1 • confidentiality - 4 • quantity - 4 • time - 2 • flow - 1	**Business Issues** • criticality - 4 • evolution - 2 • commitment - 5 • knowledge - 2

Diagrammatic representation

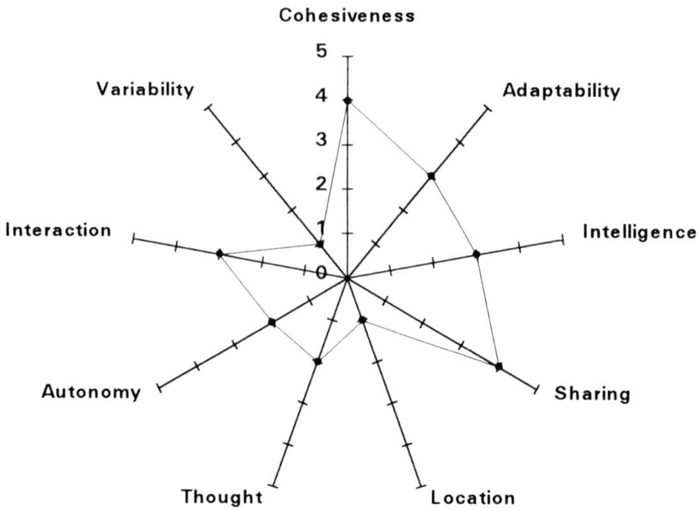

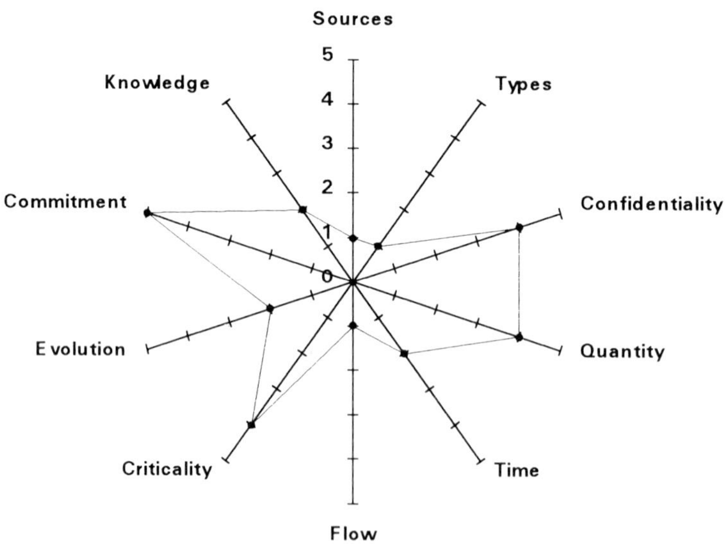

Figure 9.1 Characteristics of the work group

Conclusions

- Attributes of the work group - the work group operates well as a team (cohesiveness), consistently share information (sharing) and are located in the same place (location). Therefore, the product chosen should provide the framework for collaboration and information sharing in a local environment.
- Analysis of work group activities - the work group carries out the same activities on a daily basis (variability) and aren't very IT literate (thought) or in control of their work procedures (autonomy). Therefore the product chosen does not have to very flexible and should provide the means for strictly defined processes to be carried out.
- Properties of the information - the information processed by the group comes from a single source (sources) and is of the same type (types) - application forms through the post. The information is confidential (confidentiality) and there is a lot of it (quantity). The information does not have to be held for long periods of time (time) and there is a predefined path that it follows (flow). Therefore the product chosen does not have to be capable of handling different information types from a range of sources but must have security features and be capable of routing the information along a predefined path.
- Business Issues - The processing of the mortgage applications is semi-critical (criticality) and the management are thoroughly committed (commitment) to changing this process with the help of groupware. The process is quite stable (evolution) and the team are not that aware of the groupware concept (knowledge). Therefore the product chosen must be reliable, can be radical in thinking but not in the way that it alters working procedures and does not have to be particularly flexible.

Recommendations

The recommendation for this work group is that it adopts a workflow solution. Workflow software is perfectly suited to this type of clerical, paper shuffling activity and it can be used to fully automate the process. This involves defining the path that the information will follow and using this information to electronically route the information to those people who need it.

Workflow software is also reliable, does not change the work procedures a great deal (it just automates them), can handle vast quantities of information flowing through the system and permits effective collaboration and information sharing in a team located locally.

9.3 Matching characteristics to technologies

Once the work group characteristics have been identified, they can be used to select the most appropriate set of groupware technologies from those identified in Chapter 5. The set may merely include a single technology category but is likely to include more than one - groupware is a family of products. Each category of technology has characteristics of its own which makes it suitable for different work group and business process scenarios. The following sections give a description of the characteristics that each technology possesses and gives spider diagrams of each. These are useful when comparing the outcome of the work group analysis.

When performing the comparison between the work group and technology characteristics, you should be interested in similarities between the factors given high or low scores. Characteristics which have been given a medium score usually mean that they are not particularly important in the evaluation. Notice the similarity between the peaks and troughs of the workflow spider diagrams and those of the work group analysis given in the previous section.

9.3.1 Messaging

Messaging software includes electronic mail and conferencing facilities All successful groupware implementations require a basic form of electronic messaging facility to be available to workers so that they can communicate asynchronously.

Standard e-mail facilities support teams that require little close collaboration and the introduction of e-mail is not a big culture shock requiring commitment from managers at all levels. It is simple to use and with intelligent routing facilities built into it can provide for autonomy in the flow of information. E-mail can be sent and received from any location possessing the necessary facilities and communication links and most types of data can be attached to messages. The security of e-mail links is not appropriate for the transmission of highly confidential documents and sending vast quantities of mail tends to clog up networks.

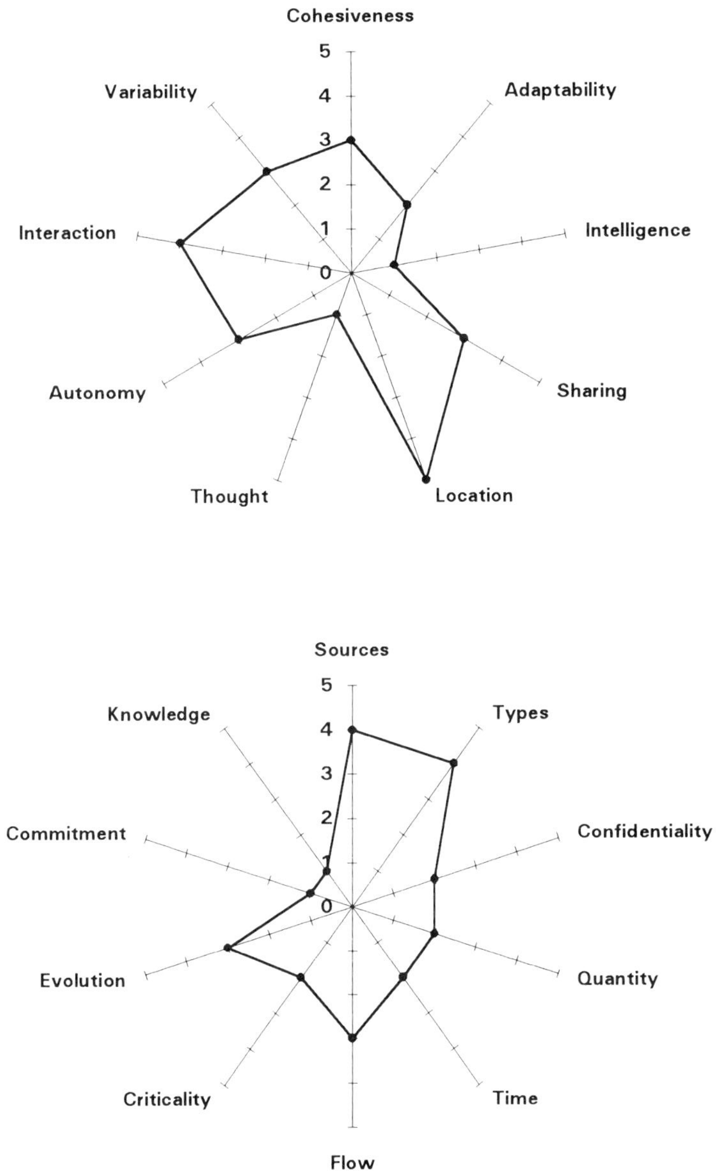

Figure 9.2 Characteristics of messaging technology

Conferencing facilities allow members of a team to communicate from remote locations synchronously, i.e., in real-time. Conferencing gives the users the feel of a real face-to-face meeting. Confidentiality is therefore not maintained but it provides remotely located teams with an effective collaboration tool. The expense of such a facility will usually require support from a senior level of management.

9.3.2 Information sharing

If collaboration, cooperation, and information sharing is imperative in a group, then some form of information sharing software will be needed. This is also the case if vast quantities of information are handled and stored by the team for long periods of time.

Document management software can be invaluable if a large number of documents are handled by a work group, especially if these have to be held for long periods of time. Document management systems (DMS) can help a work group to organise these documents efficiently so that each member always knows exactly where to look for a particular document or piece of information. Critical functions also benefit from DMS because of their automatic backup and restore facilities. This ensures that very little information is ever lost. Teams that are spread over several locations can still benefit from DMS because the software will organise documents stored anywhere on a network, be it a LAN or WAN. By controlling the permission rights of users and enforcing these during access to information, a high degree of confidentiality can be maintained. The introduction of the software does require a change in work practices because users will have to adhere to the rules put in place regarding the storage of documents.

Joint authoring products allow team members to simultaneously access documents and make changes to them, with the amendments appearing on everybody's screen in real-time. These products obviously provide for effective collaboration and interaction between team members and also allow for very effective sharing of information. The change in culture necessary to use such systems can be a hindrance as team members work is open to direct scrutiny and can be changed by anybody. If the team's work varies considerably, these systems provide a useful mechanism for allowing team members to quickly draft joint proposals, reports, memos, analysis, etc. Confidentiality is obviously an issue with such products. The location of team members is irrelevant as long as the necessary network infrastructure is in place.

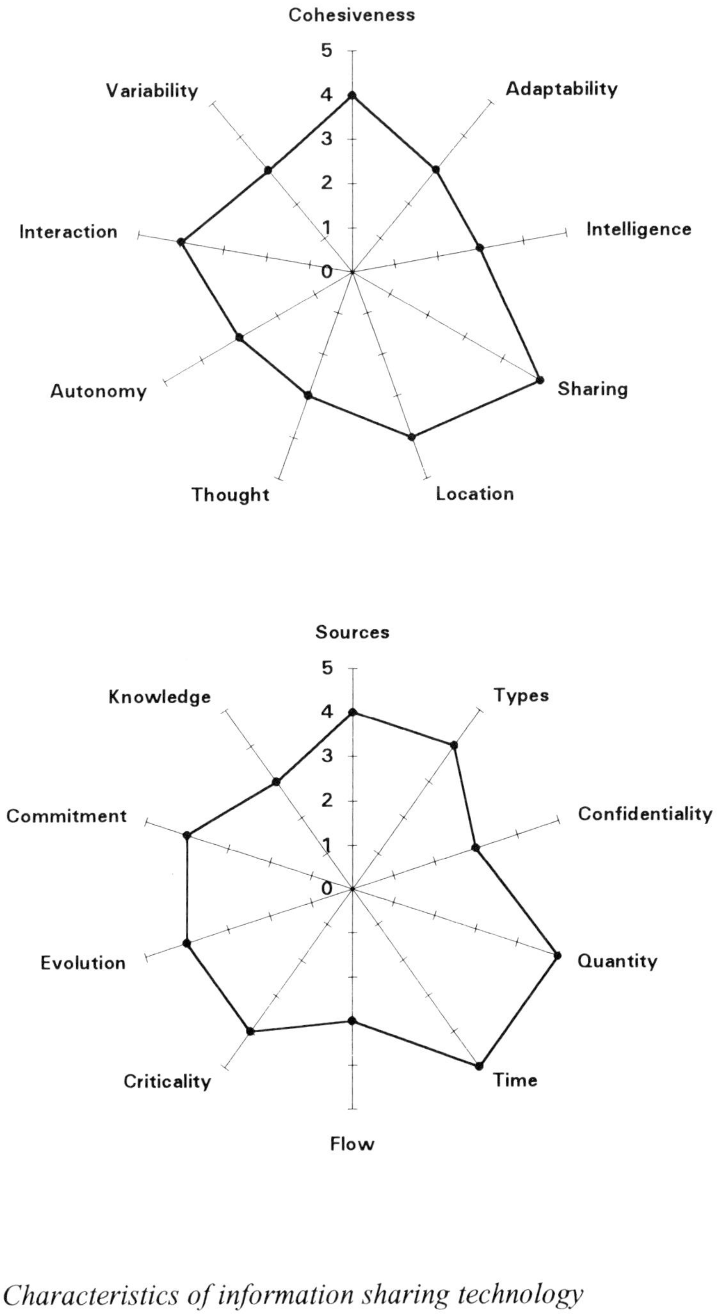

Figure 9.3 Characteristics of information sharing technology

9.3.3 Scheduling

A high degree of collaboration and cooperation within the group spells the need for scheduling software. This allows team members to check on each other's availability and to automatically schedule meetings and resources.

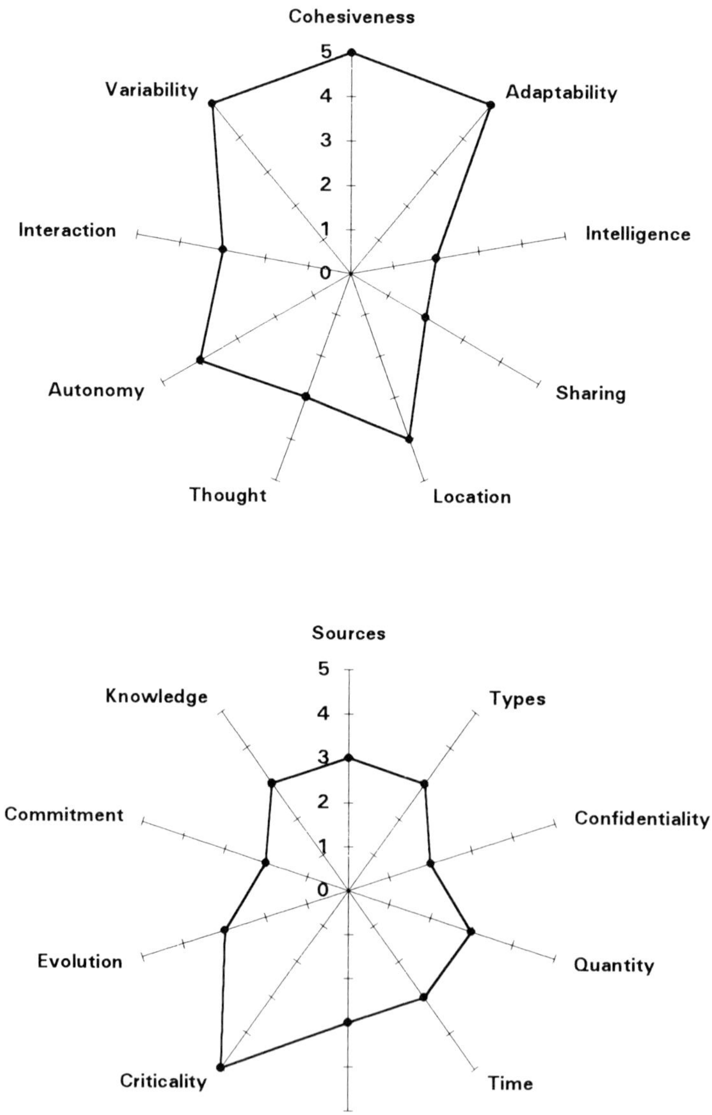

Figure 9.4 Characteristics of scheduling

Scheduling software also supports a high degree of autonomy and variability within a group by allowing them to book each other immediately for unforeseen events.

Scheduling software does require everybody to maintain personal diaries and if these are not kept up to date by everybody, the software becomes useless. A change in working practices is therefore required and if the team's processes are critical, it is imperative that the scheduling software is used correctly.

This tends to suggest that it is not appropriate for critical processes. This is true if diaries are not maintained, but if used correctly, the software can play an important role in ensuring that a group project is completed to schedule.

Scheduling software does support a certain amount of 'flow' because people and resources can be scheduled for various purposes during the life cycle of the process. It is also useful for team members in disparate locations to coordinate their activities.

9.3.4 Case / workflow management

Workflow management software is ideal for teams which process information in a predefined way with information flows rarely changing. Used intelligently, they can allow for autonomy in the team's work but mainly they will route information along a predetermined path.

Using workflow management software usually requires a change in the culture and working practices of an organisation because it can be used as an enabler for business process redesign. It will therefore require management support and commitment to provide the training and change management which will be needed. Interaction between team members will be minimal with the software controlling the passing of information between them and it does not allow a great deal of variability in day-to-day activities.

Large quantities of information can be processed through task management software and it allows users to share information queues but not actual information. The location of teams is not an issue if the appropriate network infrastructure is in place.

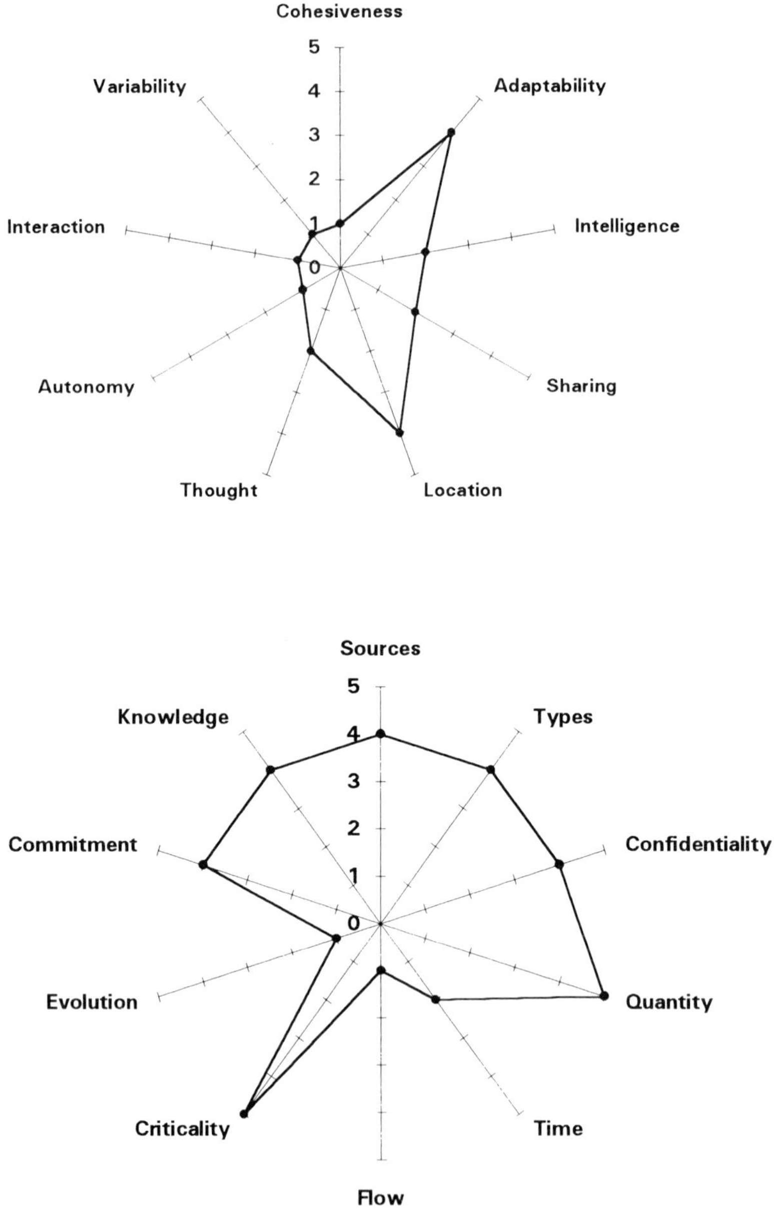

Figure 9.5 Characteristics of workflow technology

9.3.5 Group decision support systems (GDSS)

When teams require a high degree of collaboration, interaction and attend many meetings, Group Decision Support Systems can be particularly useful.

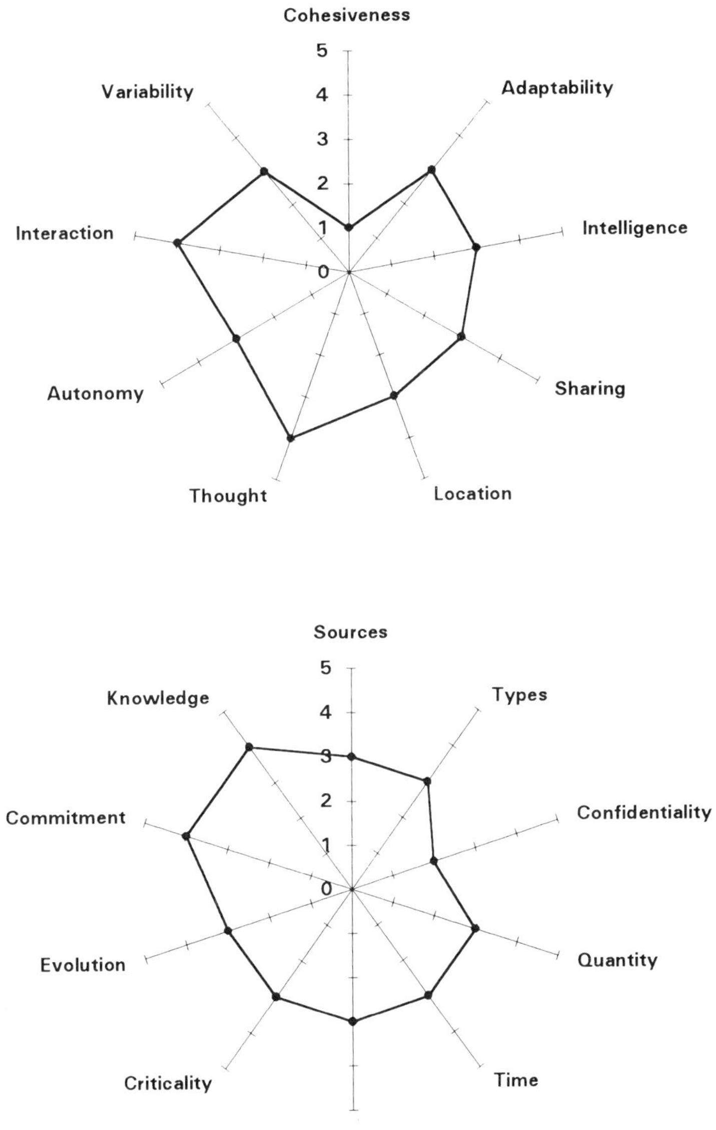

Figure 9.6 Characteristics of GDSS technology

Group Decision Support Systems provide for more effective and productive meetings. They are able to support autonomy in a team's work because they allow meetings to be called instantaneously and allow ideas and thoughts to be shared.

This property also makes Group Decision Support Systems useful in teams which are continually evolving; they can be used to help team members discuss the path of the evolution.

Using these electronic meeting tools requires people to change the way that they conduct themselves in meetings and the technology, as it is costly, will require support from senior level management. Group Decision Support Systems can be used to conduct meetings between members from remote locations although in this situation, confidentiality becomes an issue.

9.3.6 Reporting

If the team processes and stores vast quantities of information, reporting tools will be useful to allow members to extract the subsets of data that are important to them.

Reporting tools can also be used to monitor the flow of information or gather data in different formats from different sources. If the reporting tools are flexible enough, they will allow for autonomy in the group's work by allowing different information to be reported on as necessary. Reporting tools also allow information sharing as the subsets required by different team members may overlap.

In general executive information systems are very flexible and can support a continually evolving information need.

9.3.7 Summary of the selection process

The following tables provide a summary of each of the groupware technologies described in this book:

- Attributes of the work group
- Analysis of Work Group Activities
- Properties of the Information
- Business Issues

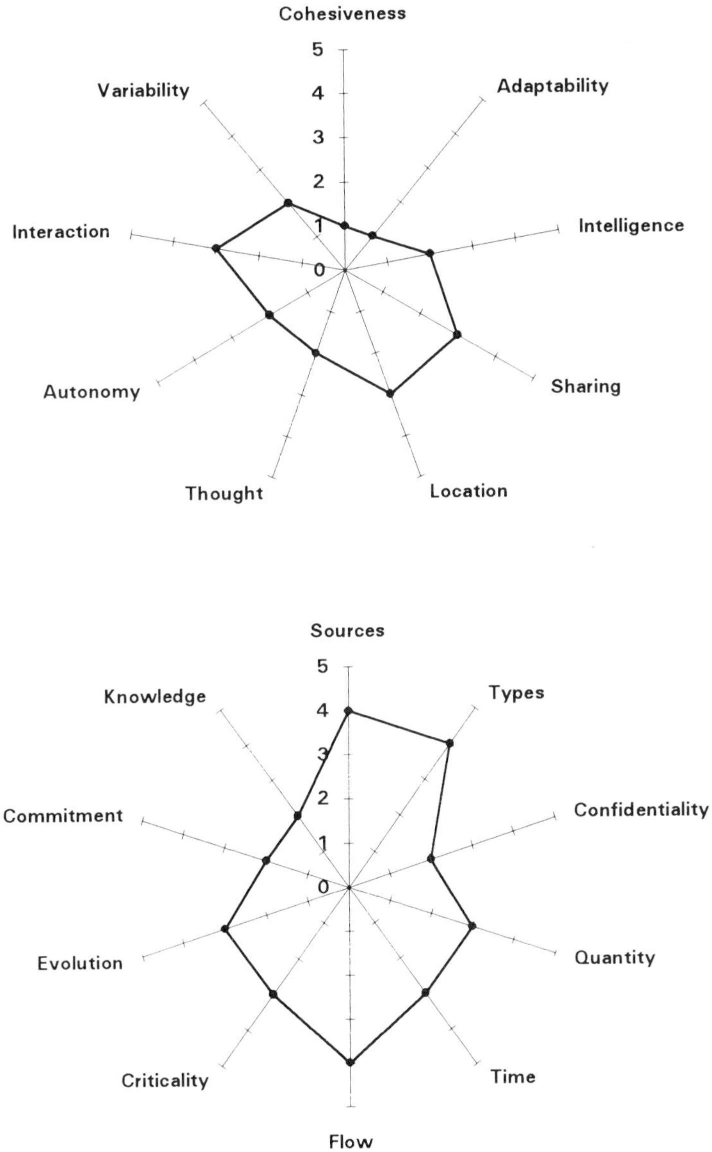

Figure 9.7 Characteristics of reporting technology

Attributes of the work group

Characteristics	*Cohesion*	*Adaptability*	*Intelligence*	*Sharing*	*Location*
E mail and conferencing	a means for the members to keep in touch	employees must use facility and regularly check mail	e mail has wide implementation base and is simple to use	documents can be transmitted and ideas shared	teams can communicate any time, any place
Information sharing	a means for teams to share information and therefore enhance cohesion	documents stored in particular locations: work may be under more scrutiny	joint authoring tools require high degree of IT knowledge	a means for information to be shared throughout the work group	information can be shared regardless of location
Electronic scheduling	allows groups to schedule activities	team members must maintain electronic diaries	medium degree of IT awareness needed	details of team members' location / plans can be shared	activities can be coordinated regardless of location
Workflow management	no requirement for cohesive team	if processes are reengineered, new procedures will be required	processes will be completely automated	information queue can be shared	can operate independent of team members' location
GDSS	no requirement for cohesive team	electronic meeting needs new meeting techniques	meetings conducted using IT	permits sharing of ideas during meetings	meetings can be conducted irrespective of location
Reporting tools	no requirement for cohesive team	no adaptability required	users must be able to interpret charts	will retrieve data subsets from organisational memory	can retrieve data from remote sources

Analysis of Work Group Activities

Characteristics	*Thought*	*Autonomy*	*Interaction*	*Variability*
E mail and conferencing	no complex thought required	allows for autonomy through information flows and intelligent routing	e-mail allows high degree of asynchronous interaction; conferencing allows face to face interaction	messages can be sent to notify groups of change occurring due to variable work
Information sharing	need to maintain organisation of data	users know where information is stored and gain autonomy	joint authoring systems permit a high degree of interaction	efficient management of information: easy to vary procedures
Electronic scheduling	teams organise themselves to complete complex tasks	a means for teams to organise themselves	does not provide direct interaction facilities	allows schedules to be changes because of varying work
Workflow management	manages information flows	manages information flows	software maintains queues of work - interaction required	automated process conforms to predefined business process
GDSS	the means for more productive meetings	electronic meetings result in more ideas being generated with greater creativity	allows for a large amount of computer mediated interaction	issues are dealt with more swiftly at electronic meetings
Reporting tools	must understand the presentation of figures	can allow teams to monitor figures and progress	not applicable	EIS s are usually very flexible

Properties of the information

Characteristics	*Sources*	*Types*	*Confidentiality*	*Quantity*	*Time*	*Flow*
E mail and conferencing	sending or receiving from any source with facilities	many document types can be attached to messages	mail boxes may not be secure; messages can be sent by mistake	large quantities of mail can clog network	not adequate to keep messages for long periods	intelligent mail applications can control simple work flow
Information sharing	can be used to share data from several sources	can share information of several types	can control access to documents	manages distribution of large amounts of information	can store information efficiently for long periods	does not support information flows
Electronic scheduling	not applicable	not applicable	team members' plans available to whole team	not applicable	not applicable	not applicable
Workflow management	can capture and route data from most sources	can capture and route any type of data	most packages have security features built in	can handle vast quantities of information	inappropriate for tasks which take long time to complete	can formally manage flow and routing of information
GDSS	not applicable	not applicable	anonymity in electronic meeting but no general confidentiality	not applicable	not applicable	not applicable
Reporting tools	can report information from any number of sources	can be used to report on information of a number of types	can restrict access depending on user types	can be used to retrieve subsets from organisational memory	can report on changes in information over time	can report on state of information during its lifecycle

Business issues

Characteristics	*Criticality*	*Evolution*	*Commitment*	*Knowledge*
E mail and conferencing	inform team members of latest developments	intelligent mail applications offer flexibility	no high degree of commitment required	no knowledge of groupware required
Information sharing	can be used to manage information in critical processes	allows flexibility in information management strategies	joint authoring requires commitment due to cost	may require some degree of groupware experience to accept changes
Electronic scheduling	critical tasks can be scheduled efficiently	not applicable	may come as standard in some office automation packages	team members will have to understand benefits of team working
Workflow management	critical tasks can be fully automated	best suited to stable processes	expense and associated reengineering require management support	users need to be convinced of benefits of groupware
GDSS	enables more effective meetings to take place	not applicable	expense will require management support	need to understand benefits of electronic meetings
Reporting tools	overview of critical business information	can monitor evolving information or processes	usually provided by senior management	need to appreciate need for organisational memory

9.4 Fitting in with the groupware pyramid principle

This section has explained the procedures which should be followed in order to build the first foundation block of the groupware pyramid. At the end of this stage, the organisation should be in a structural and cultural position to accept a groupware implementation and realise the full benefits from it. Team members should appreciate the need to work effectively in teams and should have received the necessary training and support to allow them to do so. Each team should have the responsibility of completing specific tasks where an end result is visible and members of the team should have direct contact with the customers of the service they are providing. The characteristics of the work groups and business processes should have been identified and used to select the appropriate groupware technologies.

If this is the case, the organisation is in a healthy position to successfully take up the challenge of making a groupware implementation work for them.

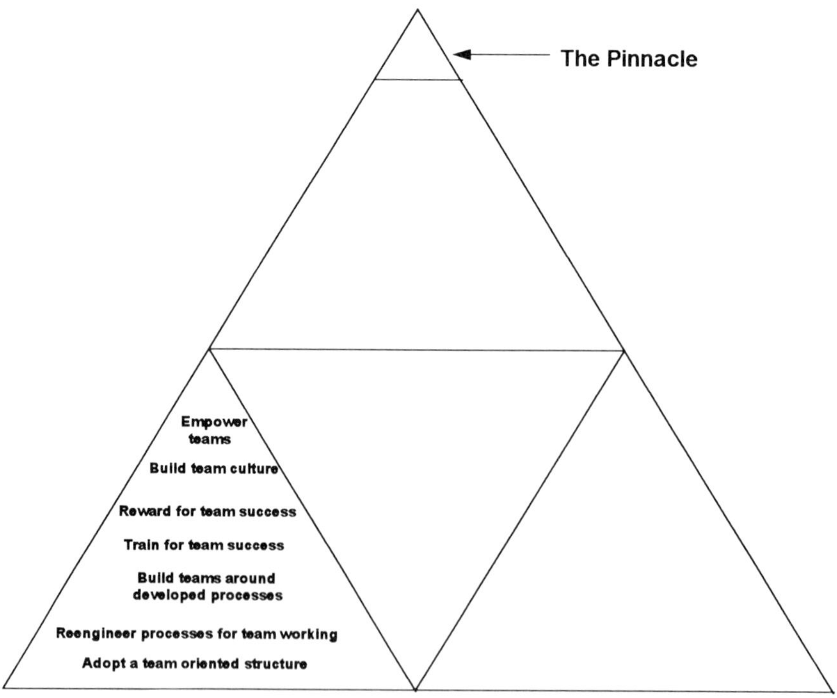

Figure 9.8 First foundation block in place

Section IV. Implementing a groupware solution

Chapter 10. Selecting a pilot system

In recent years, the take up of networking and electronic mail has meant that most organisations now have at least one Local Area Network (LAN) and some form of corporate electronic messaging system in place. Implementation of both technologies is still growing rapidly and they have probably now achieved critical mass in the market place. This is one of the reasons for the current interest in groupware technology - networking and electronic mail, along with a corporate database, are enabling technologies for a groupware implementation.

Teams need to be working on a network so that members can collaborate and communicate effectively. They also need the ability to communicate with other teams and individuals both internal and external to the organisation. Many companies use their existing infrastructure as a route into groupware by purchasing products which add simple workgroup facilities to the network. As the benefits of the groupware technology become apparent and are publicised, the implementation base usually grows throughout the organisation and may eventually result in a company-wide buy-in.

The other route into groupware is to take the revolutionary approach and use groupware to rebuild and refocus the organisation. In section III, we mentioned how groupware can be used as an enabler for business process reengineering and business restructuring. Many organisations, especially the larger ones, take this approach to get their business moving again and to beat the inertia that has set in. The risks involved with this form of implementation are significant but if it is carefully planned and managed, the benefits can be enormous.

The two main entry points for groupware are therefore:

- Adding groupware products to the existing network architecture to enhance the work group facilities. This method is a simple way to get into groupware and the introduction of products which achieve 'quick hits' - eliminate the obvious problems present in a work group - will automatically achieve user buy-in and provide the necessary stimulus to extend the implementation base further.
- Using groupware to completely restructure the organisation and redesign the processes within it. Large organisation sometimes find themselves in a state of inertia or in a dormant period where the business is not growing, employee morale is reducing and traditional techniques to remedy this situation are not working. Groupware allows organisations to get out of this damaging situation by providing a means to introduce revolutionary change.

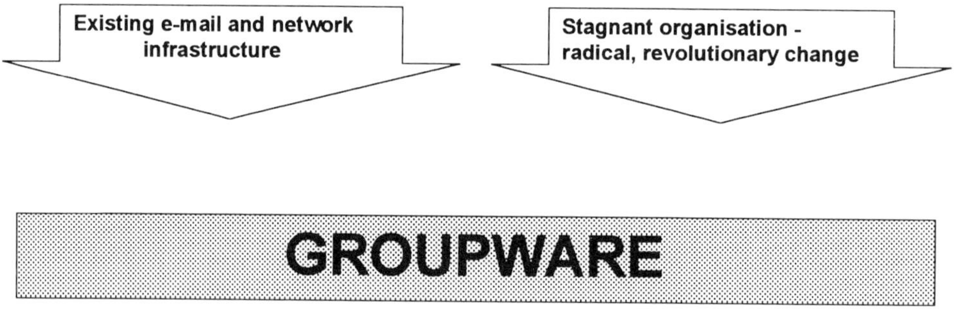

Figure 10.1 The routes into groupware

Whichever approach is used to get groupware into an organisation, it is likely that it will significantly change the way in which people work and the organisation functions. We believe that it is therefore essential that a pilot scheme is conducted to enable the organisation to:

- assess the needs of the work groups
- educate the employees as to the benefits of groupware
- achieve comprehensive user buy-in
- identify the problems that may appear in a large scale implementation
- be able to measure the benefits of the initial investment and provide justification for a wider implementation.

10.1 Start small

Most groupware gurus advocate the policy of 'Start small, grow big' where groupware is concerned. The main reasons for the widespread support of this policy are:

- Groupware is a new technology which is not widely understood by the user and management population. Its introduction must therefore be accompanied by an education programme which informs the users and, perhaps more importantly at first, management of its wide range of benefits. A well planned and implemented pilot scheme gives the opportunity for an organisation to begin this education programme. If the pilot is targeted at a specific business function with several quick hits in mind, the significant benefits which will be achieved can be publicised and used to convince users that groupware will change their lives for the better.
- Groupware is a new technology which has had very few major implementations across the breadth of large organisations. There are not a great number of case studies from which to learn and those that have been published usually appear in marketing material and therefore concentrate on promoting the benefits of the implementation. The effects of a groupware invasion are still widely unknown, especially the long term effects, and it is therefore sensible to start small and observe these effects without too much strain or risk being put on the organisation.
- Groupware is a new technology but there are an abundance of products which claim to fall under the groupware umbrella. Selecting the right product for your organisation or for a work group is vital if the full benefits of team working are to be realised. The methodology in the previous section gives very useful guidance as to which form of groupware technology would be appropriate but selecting a product from within a technology group can pose a larger problem. Pilot schemes provide the opportunity to test a number of products and assess the benefits of each relative to the needs of the organisation.

The implementation of groupware is a major step and will cause great upheaval in an organisation. The strain put on employees and business processes must be planned for and adequately dealt with. Jones and

Kaye [*Jones and Kaye 1993*] believe that groupware is unlikely to initially replace existing OA systems on a company-wide scale, but will instead evolve from a handful of strategically chosen sites. They go on to say

> "... more likely, PC LAN users will probably, as they did with PCs in the first place, install groupware themselves and let the rest of the corporation follow. This will either upgrade OA systems to handle a variety of clients, or ultimately shift entirely to a network of smaller LANs linked over WANs with groupware software".

They are advocating pilot schemes by suggesting that groupware should evolve from a handful of strategic sites. The point that they make about groupware being implemented by PC LAN users with the rest of the organisation catching up afterwards is a very possible scenario and causes the authors considerable concern. The very substantial impact that groupware will necessarily have on an organisation requires that the implementation should be ultimately planned and managed from a central corporate IT function or from departmental IT functions with feedback and monitoring from a corporate division.

The problems of incompatibility between PCs, LANs, software, communications systems and hardware that is now being experienced in many organisations as they attempt to eradicate their legacy of information management, prove that groupware must not be allowed to sneak in via the backdoor. If departments are to implement groupware solutions, this needs to be under the control of some central function. This will ensure that when the time comes for a company wide implementation, the organisation will not be faced with a mish-mash of products, sitting on a variety of machines, accessing a variety of data stores and supporting a variety of communications and other standards. If departmental functions are given a free rein where groupware is concerned, future compatibility problems will become a major issue and will inevitably provide another opportunity for software suppliers to cash in by providing add on products to combat the compatibility problems.

10.2 Selecting the appropriate pilot system

We, and many groupware experts, agree that the best and least risk ridden route into a groupware solution is to start small and grow big. Targeting a specific business function or department, realising and publicising the benefits from this and spreading the implementation to other parts of the business is the most appropriate method for a groupware implementation. Groupware has the habit of seeding itself into an organisation and a well planned pilot project can act as a significant fertiliser in this process. Before the fertiliser can be applied the implementation must have firm roots, providing a stable base on which groupware can blossom.

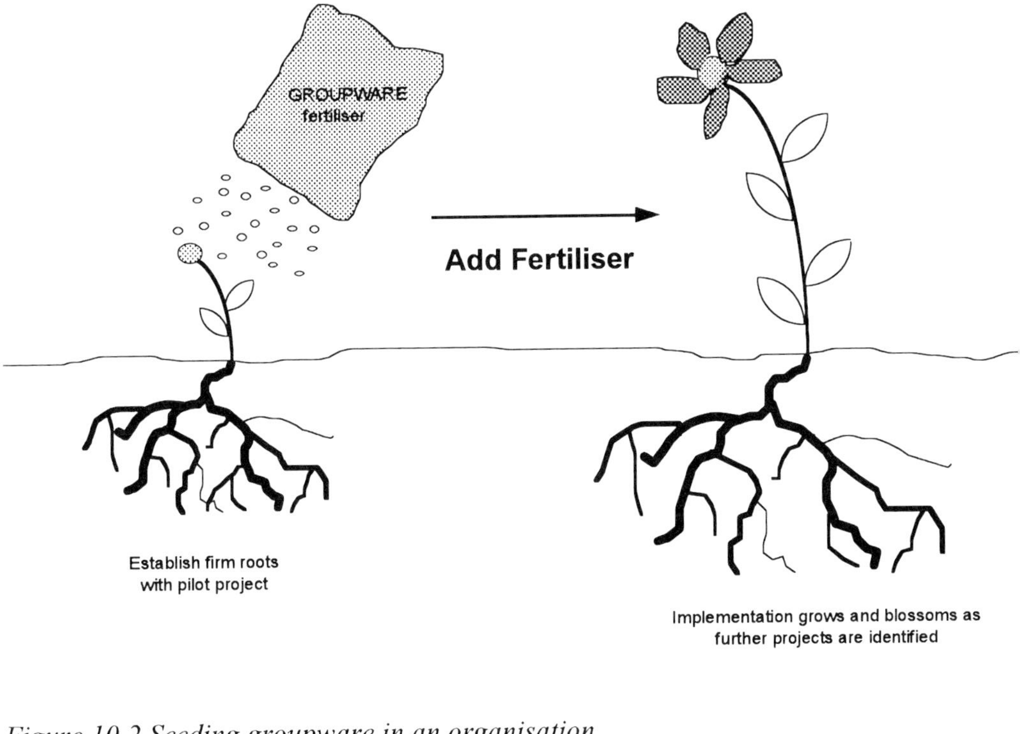

Figure 10.2 Seeding groupware in an organisation

There are a number of steps which need to be taken to implement a successful groupware pilot project:

- identify an area of the business which would benefit significantly from groupware and select a pilot scheme
- find a champion or sponsor

- produce a benefits plan outlining the gains that are expected from the pilot and outline a timetable for the implementation and evaluation procedure
- select the appropriate team for the pilot project
- identify the characteristics of the team and the processes they will be required to carry out and select the appropriate groupware product
- produce a design for the pilot project
- define any necessary working or best practices and procedures for the pilot scheme
- train users in preparation for the system and market the objectives of the pilot to other members of the organisation
- implement the pilot
- continue training and supporting the users
- perform a constructive evaluation of the pilot against the benefits plan established at the outset
- publicise the success of the pilot - leave the organisation in a excited state of anticipation.

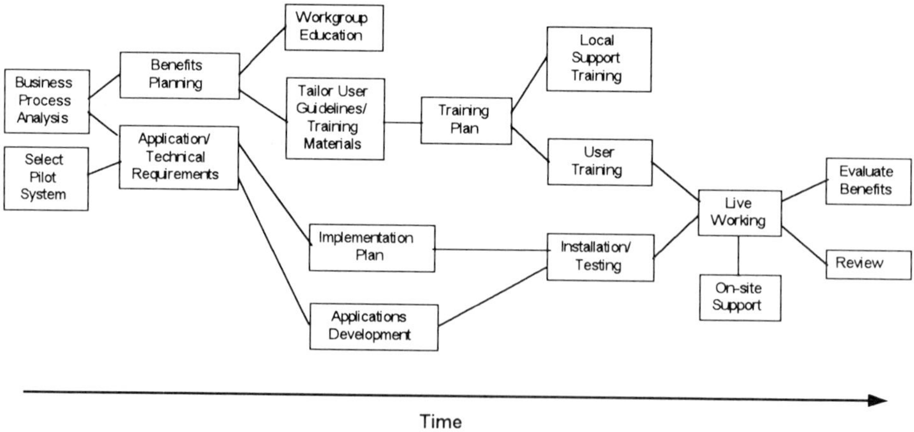

Figure 10.3 Flow chart of a groupware implementation

10.3 Identify the pilot project

The real aims of a pilot project are to prove that the introduction of groupware into an organisation will realise significant benefits. This is in addition to identifying the potential problems of a larger implementation and gaining the opportunity to test a number of groupware products. To prove that groupware can provide tangible and justifiable benefits, the pilot project must be such that the introduction of the technology will have a significant impact and provide obvious and measurable benefits immediately.

The pilot project needs to be centred around a business process, function or department that has a considerable level of 'pain' in the work it is carrying out. If the areas and causes of this 'pain' can be identified, groupware can be implemented to relieve it or completely eradicate it - groupware should be used as a pain release mechanism.

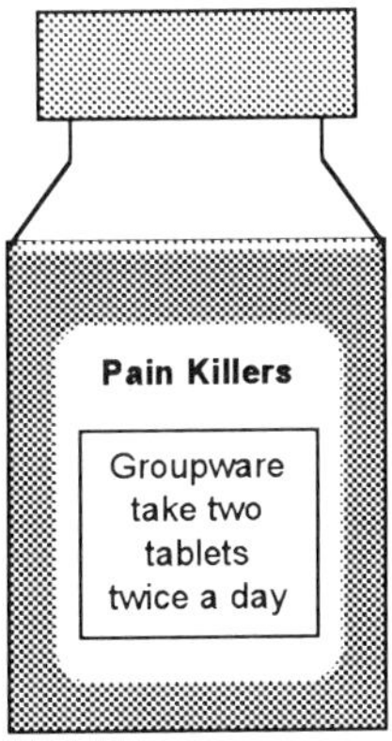

Figure 10.4 Groupware is an effective pain killer

It is our experience that typical pilot schemes have the following characteristics:

- They are implemented in areas of the business that are not critical to the functioning of the organisation. This ensures that should the pilot be a disaster, the organisation as a whole will not suffer. This means that pilots are usually conducted on an internal, non-critical business process.
- They centre around a business function or department that is involved in a largely paper shuffling process where information is vital but rarely immediately available.

- They concentrate on areas where team work is essential and communication and collaboration between team members is important.
- They sometimes run alongside and in parallel with the existing system so that the differences can be identified, measured and the users fully understand and appreciate the benefits of the new system.
- They are conducted in areas where the 'pain level' of the current process is high and groupware can act as a immediate and effective pain killer.

We believe that there are obvious candidate pilot groupware schemes in every organisation and this is perhaps the cause of the problem in selecting one. There are so many areas where groupware can have a significant impact that selecting the most appropriate one is virtually impossible. There are many other factors which will affect the choice of pilot and may help to reduce the number of possibilities:

- Cost - groupware is not a particularly cheap option and gaining a large budget for a pilot scheme will probably not be possible. Costs will have to be kept to a minimum which may rule out certain pilots which would require a large investment to be undertaken.
- Available groupware technology - with groupware still being a relatively new technology, there are many promises being made by software vendors with regard to new and revolutionary technology which they are about to release. Many of the products which are being promised are merely vapourware - software that we are told will appear and never actually does - with vendors trying to improve their image in the market place. Pilot schemes should not be chosen under the assumption that such vapourware products will actually appear.
- Available corporate technology - to be successful groupware requires that the organisation have an appropriate IT infrastructure in place. This should, as a minimum, consist of high speed PCs connected via reliable and efficient networks with available support and maintenance facilities. The limitations of departments in this area may rule some out of a pilot implementation.

- Personnel - the team that is chosen to take part in the pilot scheme will play an important part in its success. They must be IT literate, be willing and adaptable to change and be enthusiastic and committed to achieving success. Selection of the pilot team is covered in greater detail below.

10.3.1 Typical pilot projects

From the experience that we have gained in the implementation of pilot groupware schemes and from the documented case studies presented in the literature, there are certain business functions which seem to be appropriate and popular candidates for a pilot project:

Internal help desk function

The internal software and hardware help desk support is an ideal candidate for a groupware pilot. An existing system will already be in place for the logging and monitoring of user problems and this may be paper based. The personnel in this area will be highly IT literate and will be working in a team, sharing their knowledge and experiences to help solve user problems. They will probably keep up with the latest IT trends and therefore understand about groupware and its benefits. This will mean that they will be enthusiastic about a possible groupware implementation and will want it to succeed. There is often a high pain level in this type of function as help desks usually have service level agreements which they must meet and this will involve logging, monitoring and escalating user problems. Groupware can assist in the help desk process by:

- providing a central repository of help desk knowledge which can be accessed by all the help desk team to assist them in their problem solving activities. This can also be used to maintain a software and hardware inventory (information sharing technology).
- helping team members to cooperate and communicate more effectively by providing messaging facilities, perhaps remote, so that each team member is always contactable (messaging technology).
- automating the flow of user problems and queries from the stage of receiving the call to logging and monitoring its progress through the system. This could also involve the automatic escalation of

problems which have passed the service level agreement times (workflow management technology).

- providing accurate, timely and informative reports on the help desk database. This will allow the help desk to identify common problems and take measures to reduce these (reporting technology).
- give the help desk team the facilities to jointly work on the reports that provide solutions to major IT problems (joint authoring technology).

Personnel department

The personnel department of an organisation is another ideal candidate for a pilot scheme. It is semi customer-facing, in that potential employees get their first impressions of a company by their interaction with the personnel function, but it is not so critical to business success as to rule out a pilot groupware scheme. There is often a high pain level in the personnel division because applications are received in paper form and usually have to follow pre-defined paths through to the applicant's rejection or acceptance. This path can result in the loss of the application and the subsequent embarrassment of the applicant receiving no response or being asked to re-submit their CV.

The personnel process also requires a great deal of collaboration between members of the division when applicants are being considered. Opinions must be sought and short-lists drawn up, selection meetings must be held and review meetings conducted. There are many possibilities for groupware:

- the pre-defined flow of paper application forms through the department means that routing software can be employed to automate this process (workflow management software).
- the number of meetings that have to be conducted, perhaps across disparate locations with remote personnel functions and managers, means that much time is spent in the meeting room. Electronic meeting room technology can help in this process, reducing the time spent in meetings and the time and costs involved in travelling to remote meetings (GDSS).
- with the large number of meetings conducted, arranging these meetings will probably take a long time. Scheduling the people and resources for interview sessions will also be a cause of frustration.

Electronic personal organisers and scheduling software can provide help in this area by allowing meetings to be automatically arranged and resources booked (scheduling and diary management software).

- techniques used in the interviewing process sometimes involve group tests and similar activities. Meeting room technology such as electronic brainstorming tools can provide the means by which dominant individuals do not take over in group discussions, giving everybody equal opportunity to impress (GDSS).

These are just two generic functions which we have used to highlight the impact that groupware can have. There will be different problems in every organisation and a number of possible processes that would benefit from groupware. The examples merely show how groupware can be used in any organisation that has a personnel or help desk function.

Chapter 11. Building the pilot system

Once an appropriate pilot project has been identified, the road to implementation can begin. The most important point to note as an organisation sets out on this route is that user involvement from the very beginning is essential if the pilot system is to be accepted by the user population and considered a success.

11.1 Implementing the pilot system

There are many stages that have to be completed in the implementation of the pilot system.

11.1.1 Find a champion or sponsor

Groupware will change the way that an organisation operates and therefore from the outset of a groupware project, an executive or similarly senior sponsor is required. They must be of a sufficiently high level of decision making and power to be able to initiate the changes to business processes and structure which are necessary and to sanction the appropriate budget. As groupware will have effects immediately visible to higher echelons of management, commitment must be sought from this level.

There are many examples of groupware projects which, part way through implementation, have been curbed by higher levels of management who suddenly became concerned that their authority and position would be adversely affected by the results of total information sharing and team empowerment. Sponsorship must be from the top and all managers affected by the implementation must fully understand the potential impact that it will have. The executive sponsor must be prepared to take responsibility for the project and be held accountable for it. The sponsor should also be willing to extend the pilot system, should it be a success, and see the implementation through to the corporate buy-in stage.

Senior Management Sponsorship

- to initiate changes in business processes and working practices
- to sanction appropriate budget
- to understand the impact that groupware may have

Middle Management Sponsorship

- to understand the potential change in their roles
- to convey enthusiasm to the teams

User Population Sponsorship

- to accept new working procedures
- to understand benefits of groupware
- to buy-in to the new system

Figure 11.1 Sponsorship required from all levels

Sponsorship must also be achieved throughout the whole organisation. If sponsorship is just from the top, employees will be made to feel as if the technology is being forced upon them. Acceptance must be gained from the end-users so that they have a part to play in their ultimate destiny. This can be achieved by forming user groups, by producing educational and promotional newsletters or by holding meetings where users can express their concerns.

11.1.2 Produce a benefits plan and timetable

The pilot system must aim to deliver real, tangible business benefits which can be used as justification for a more widespread groupware implementation. It is quite likely that the pilot system will encounter a few problems; the technology is new and the concept of groupware not widely understood. This may lead to the goals of the pilot changing throughout the implementation until at worst, the only goal is to get the groupware software up and running. If this becomes the case, the pilot will be a disaster and be viewed as a complete waste of time. It wouldn't have been though - if a pilot had not been conducted and the implementation was on a larger scale to begin with, even more damage would have been done.

To prevent goals, aims and priorities changing during the implementation of the pilot system, it is necessary to define expectations beforehand. This means that they are always available to review and can be used additionally in the post evaluation procedure. The expectations should be both qualitative and quantitative and should be specific so that they can be measured against. Imprecise expectations such as 'we want to provide a better internal help desk service' are not specific enough to enable justifiable business benefits to be measured. Much better would be 'we want to respond to each priority one problem within one working day'. Expectations should be demanding but feasible and measurable. They should be SMARTED objectives:

- Specific - they should outline specific objectives
- Measurable - they should provide measurable results
- Achievable - they must be achievable but also demanding
- Realistic - the objectives must be achievable using the available software
- Timely - they must be achievable within a given time frame
- Educational - the pilot should be a learning experience
- Demanding - they must bring the best out of everybody.

If a list of expectations is produced, they can also be used to promote the new technology to the team of employees. Being told that the new technology will allow them to meet the expectations will help to gain their commitment and enthusiasm.

It is also important to establish a timetable and milestones for the project. This will allow the developers to know if they are falling behind and means that the milestones can be celebrated along the way. As with the expectations, the timetable should be demanding but realistic - it should not be too tight because the pilot will require many fundamental changes in the business processes and in the working practices of the employees. Failing to meet deadlines reduces morale and they should therefore be fairly lenient and achievable even after encountering a number of problems.

11.1.3 Select the appropriate team

The team that are to use the pilot project will play a very important role in its success - 'a groupware system is only as good as its least committed user' [*Bartram and Youett 1993*]. To increase the likelihood of success, the team should possess the following characteristics:

- enthusiastic - they must realise the deficiencies in the current way of working and be committed and enthusiastic to change these for the better
- end-users - they should be a group of end-users similar to those who would be using the groupware system if it were implemented on a wider scale
- IT literate - there will not be a great deal of time to train the users of the pilot about the intricacies of the particular groupware product which is chosen and they need to be able to cope with this
- adaptable and responsive to change - the pilot scheme is likely to drastically change the way that they work and they must be adaptable enough to accept this change and be positively responsive to it
- good team players - if the users have previously worked in an isolated environment, they must be the type of people who will adapt well to operating in a team environment.

11.1.4 Identify the characteristics of the team

In chapter 9, we described a method which can be used to analyse the characteristics of a work group and the associated business processes. The results of this analysis can help to select the appropriate groupware technology. This method should be used during the pilot to assist in the process of product selection - the product chosen is essential if all the objectives are to be met and significant benefits gained.

11.1.5 Produce a design for the pilot

It is likely that the pilot system will have to be implemented fairly quickly, using the existing IT infrastructure and within a limited budget. The design of the system is one of the key factors that will determine the success of the pilot as it must produce demonstrable benefits within the restrictions given above. The design of the pilot will undoubtedly need to be reviewed at several stages throughout the implementation and this means that it has to be flexible and adaptable to change with little expense or associated time penalties.

11.1.6 Define working procedures

During the implementation of the pilot, it is important that every step is taken to realise all the potential benefits. Defining working practices and procedures which can be followed by the work group will not only help them to become productive more quickly but will also help in the training process. Examples of best practices are:

- designing directory structures for file servers and local PC drives and specifying which type of information, for example public or private, data or software, etc., can be stored in which directories. This means that everybody within the team will know exactly where to look for data when they need to.
- specifying that everybody should check their electronic mail box at least two times a day. This measure ensures that users do not stop using the messaging systems because recipients are not reading their mail.
- any amendments made to a person's work are documented in a specified format so that everybody is aware of the changes and the initiator of these.
- establishing a security policy so that the integrity and confidentiality of any data is maintained. This also helps to give users confidence that any private data they may have will remain private.

Best practices will be specific for the particular business function but these examples give an idea of the type of procedures which should be put in place

11.1.7 Educate and train users

In chapter 8, we concentrated on the training that users must be given to prepare them for working in a team, i.e., the interpersonal and team building exercises. This type of training needs to be given to the pilot team members along with training for the specific system. Training needs to be given prior to the pilot system being rolled out so that when it is, the users are fully prepared for it and can become productive immediately.

Figure 11.2 Complementary training is required

It is important that training is not given too far in advance of the pilot implementation because the users will soon forget what they've learned and will only have to be re-trained when the time comes.

While the pilot users are being trained, a company wide education programme needs to be run whereby other employees are educated about groupware, the changes that it will bring to the organisation and also the benefits that it will deliver. Employees asking the question 'what's in it for me?', must know the answer and be prepared and excited about a subsequent implementation.

11.1.8 Implement the pilot

If all the preparation for the pilot has been performed, the actual implementation should be a relatively simple affair and should run smoothly. The keys to success will be that the correct infrastructure is in place to allow the system to run efficiently, that the appropriate groupware software has been chosen and that the users have been trained and educated to the level where they can exploit the full potential of the pilot system.

Users will need to be supported during the initial stages of the migration to the new system and help should always be close at hand. However good the training has been, users will undoubtedly have problems using the system for real and will almost certainly have difficulties changing their working culture and practices. Users must not be left alone during the initial stages and must feel confident that help is always available. It is also possible that they will require further training in the areas where they are experiencing particular distress.

Some users may start to fear the change once they have made the migration and any such fears must be tackled immediately as they have a habit of spreading quickly and causing significant damage to the team and the success of the project.

11.2 Developing and evaluating the pilot system

Once the implementation is complete, the pilot system must be developed further. The users cannot be left to get on with it but must be continually supported and receive additional training if required. Milestones must be celebrated when they are reached, for example, when a significant step has been made in achieving one of the goals and tweaking of the software and working practices may be required.

Once the time frame for the pilot comes to an end, a constructive evaluation must be performed to identify the benefits and publicise the success.

11.2.1 Continue training and supporting the users

During the initial stages of the migration to the pilot system, users will require much 'hand holding' and this will probably demand the dedicated services of a few specialists. Once users have come to terms with their new working environment and the new system, such dedicated help will become unnecessary.

It is at this stage that a help desk type function needs to be established. This should provide help services to the users so that they are still confident that any problems they encounter will be resolved although perhaps not as quickly as when they had the dedicated support.

As the system becomes more familiar to the users and they begin to test its capabilities, the areas in which further training is needed will become obvious. Training courses should be made available to users so that they can assess their own requirements and attend the courses if they feel the need. This approach fits in which the empowering scheme which gives users the autonomy to make their own decisions about areas such as training and development.

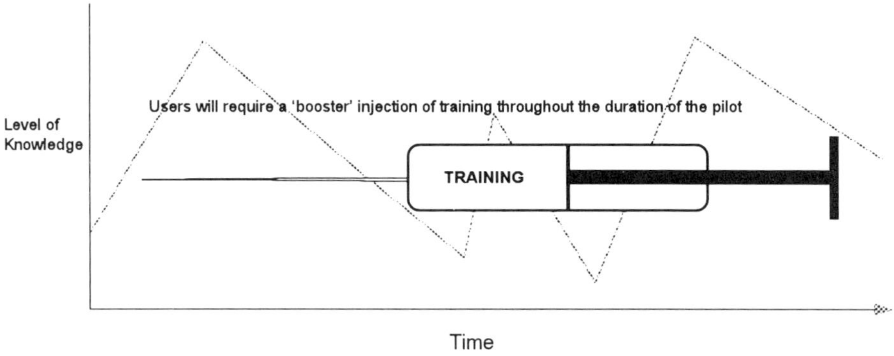

Figure 11.3 Users need 'booster training'

It is also useful to hold workshops at different stages of the product so that users can air their views and concerns about the system and their new way of working. Workshops of this type are useful because they:

- help to identify areas where greater consideration needs to be given if the pilot is extended into other areas of the business
- give users the chance to air their views and concerns. This gives them the feeling that they are an integral part of the project and that their voice is being heard
- give the opportunity to tackle the fears that users may have
- identify problems with the pilot that can be changed to meet the objectives set out in the benefits plan
- celebrate any milestones that have been reached and commit the users to reaching the next one.

11.2.2 Perform a constructive evaluation

The time will come when an evaluation of the pilot must be performed and the benefits of it measured. If a benefits plan was drawn up at the outset of the project, this task will be much more simple. The evaluation will provide the justification for the expense of the pilot and also for the implementation of groupware on a wider scale within the organisation. The evaluation process is therefore no time to be modest. Every tangible benefit that can be measured must be included.

Qualitative benefits should also be reported. The users should be interviewed to discover how they felt about the system and the change in working practices and culture - improved employee morale and collaboration are important business benefits. Also, those employees who represented the customers for the pilot process should be interviewed to discover if a better service was being provided. The biggest qualitative test is perhaps to ask the users if they would go back to their old way of working - the 'would you swap the new system for two of the old ones?' question.

The evaluation should be made against the initial benefits plan with measurements given as to how the pilot system met the specified objectives. The next section of the book gives some guidelines for measuring the benefits of a groupware implementation and for justifying further projects.

11.2.3 Publicise the success of the pilot

Hopefully the pilot system will be a great success and achieve benefits well in excess of those specified in the benefits plan. The success must be publicised throughout the entire organisation so that everybody becomes aware of groupware and the wide range of benefits that are associated with it - nothing ensures success more than feeling good about your success. Celebrating the success and initiating plans to implement groupware into other areas of the business will leave most employees in a state of welcome anticipation. If the pilot project has been extremely successful, the rest of the organisation will know about it and most users will be requesting that they be given access to similar facilities.

11.3 The groupware pyramid principle

Implementing a pilot project is the second stage of the groupware pyramid principle and once a successful pilot has been conducted, the benefits have been measured and publicised and a justifiable business case can be made for a widespread groupware implementation, the pilot system can be expanded to cover other areas of the business.

The pilot system must be implemented in an area of the business that has a high pain level and it must aim to provide quick hits and pain release immediately. This will ensure that the users buy into the system and that measurable benefits can be reported.

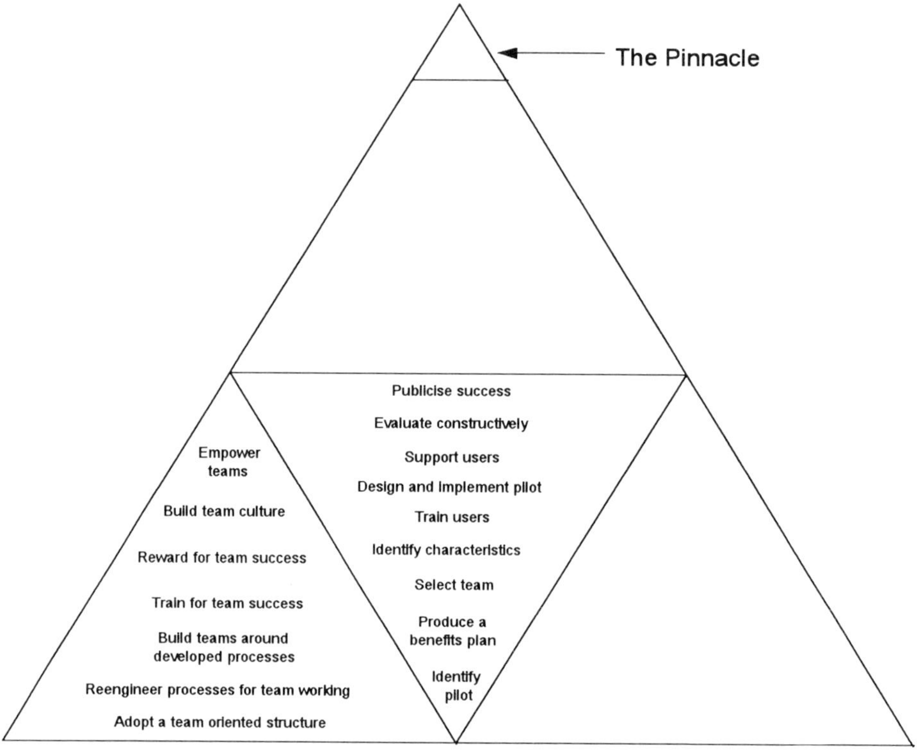

Figure 11.4 Two foundation blocks in place

Section V. Infrastructure and groupware - the technology relationship

Chapter 12. Relationship between infrastructure and a workgroup solution

The next ten years will be a decade of rapid change in the economic, political and competitive environments. Organisations will adjust by changing their business architecture, organisations, policies, practices and decision methodologies. Information technology organisations will realign their IT architectures to support the emerging business structures, selecting from a long list of developing technologies, thereby effectively discarding the most fundamental computing paradigms of the last two decades. This will have a profound effect on the end user community.

During this period of change it will be necessary that an information system to support a groupware enabled organisation is defined directly from the business strategy. The information system is a representation of information management, presentation and processing which can be facilitated through the use of technology. Information technology is the engineering realisation of the information system. However, there is a relationship between the business strategy and the technology.

12.1 Change management

Business strategy and technology can and must change in response to independent developments. However, by interacting with each other, changes can occur which are mutually beneficial. Instances of this can be seen in the way in which certain technologies have become standardised rather than being continually advanced. Other instances are becoming prevalent where business processes are being revised to take greater benefit from the new technologies.

An instance of how technical focus has moved away from operating systems and towards the packaging of business applications is in the mass market created by the spread of work stations. Engineers would not hold either MS-Windows or Unix as the ultimate in small system operating environments but they have stabilised and standardised in order to allow applications to be developed for greater user benefit.

The advent of technologies for expert systems, networking and work flow have led some corporations into changing their processes and organisations to re-group around technical solutions which can support better ways of working. This is an instance of business transformation driven by a realisation of technical benefit applied to the work place. Many of the instances of implemented groupware solutions are examples of this interaction. The introduction of many new technologies into an organisation all of which have to be integrated to provide a viable entity require the application of standards. In the same way that trains with different wheel gauges and carriage dimensions cannot be integrated into a unified transport system, nor can information technology components with different standards be integrated into a unified system.

12.2 Standardisation towards a unifying infrastructure

The trend towards standardisation started with hardware and operating systems but has continued a pace into open system initiatives which embrace broad areas of computer and communication technologies. It is now possible and indeed desirable to seek a unifying infrastructure. Such an infrastructure would include all the industry standard interfaces and support tools which will drive towards greater concentration upon technologies which directly relate to information system imperatives. This, therefore must becomes the goal of most far sighted corporations where the importance of correct manipulation of information and productive processes are paramount in delivering business benefit.

For any organisation setting out to develop a groupware solution it is important to set information system requirements in the context of business strategy.

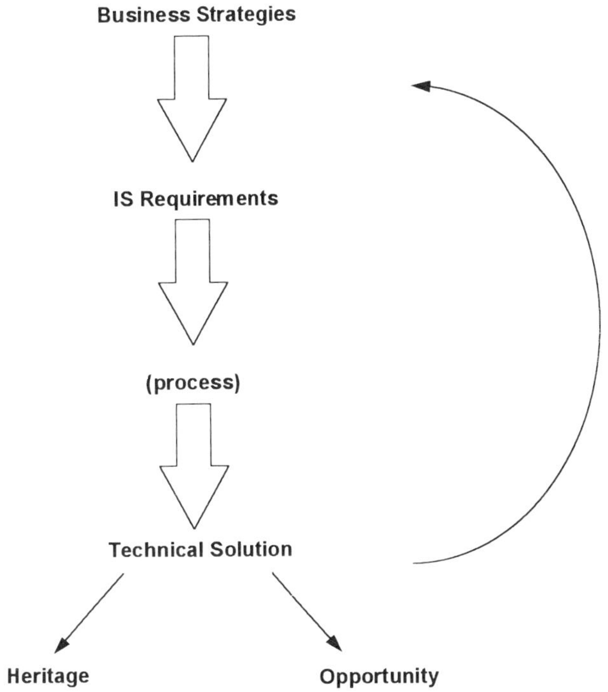

Figure 12.1 Matching technology with IS requirements

It is also important to be open to technical opportunity. These opportunities should be speedily realised and appraised objectively. To this end, business goals and organisational policies should be articulated and technology research and development carefully monitored. Processes to bring these influences together should be part of the way in which the information system requirements are stated and the information technology defined. The whole process of achieving best fit between what is needed and what is possible will have to be part of an on-going alignment programme. This programme will have a number of stages.

12.3 Concept of an architecture model

The way in which information technology comes together in a design to satisfy the information system requirements is defined by the system architecture. Architecture for information systems defines the layout and structure of all the components and describes the way in which they interact.

Information system architectures can be expressed in a variety of ways to match different points of observation In order to create and retain a universal perception of the information system architecture, two concepts are important.

- Shared graphical representations of the system,
- More than one viewpoint of analysis.

Many viewpoints are possible and indeed valid, dependent upon what needs to be 'seen'. For example, a system manager may wish to trace end-user access paths from a security viewpoint or diagnose the network and disc traffic from a system response point of view. Again, a programmer may wish to view the system as a sequential processing environment, seeking to control and observe interfaces with operational support systems.

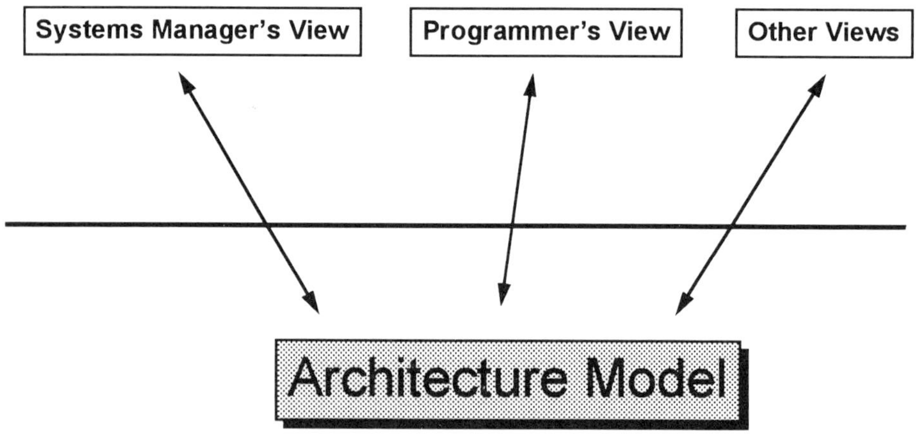

Figure 12.2 There are many views of an architecture

Dynamic process state changes offer a different 'picture' of system operation to that presented by analysis of the data structure. Representation of these situations is normally assisted by graphical means. Many valid models of architecture exist and it is important to choose one or more complementary models as the standard by which to define and measure an architecture. This is necessary when implementing a groupware solution since many components are involved.

12.3.1 Groupware applications sit within the architecture

Groupware applications sit within the architecture and on top of the infrastructure. Infrastructure provides hardware and software which make up the delivery platform and sustain an effective development and technical support environment.

Infrastructure provides the means to enable business applications and to integrate the whole information system, both locally and across networks. It is a complex technical design domain upon which depends the flexibility and capability of data and application usage.

The terms 'data architecture' and 'application architecture' have been coined to define important and complementary ways to analyse a system architecture. Both these approaches have obvious business importance. The data architecture maps where the data lives, who owns it and how it is moved, copied and updated. The application architecture takes a view of the system which looks at the sequence of processing, any parallelism which exists, the interfaces and passing of control between tasks. There is a need for a consistent approach to application architecture and this is controlled by the development environment. Organisations should set out and publish the technical policies and standards needed for both the run-time and development environments.

If the infrastructure fails to provide a development environment, (e.g., SQL, language compilers) the resulting application software may not work well within the architecture at run-time. This is a problem that many early implementations of groupware have incurred.

12.3.2 Multiple stack infrastructure

An information system architecture for most organisations consists of a number of different technologies. Sometimes these technologies have been successfully integrated within a shared development and run-time environment. But often, they consist of sub-systems which have been tailored to exhibit different characteristics (e.g., a transaction processing system or a batch-oriented MIS system). In this latter case, the overall system may be an amalgam of sub-systems which present only high level interfaces with each other and are otherwise separate processing environments, sometimes with their own data-bases. So that these separate environments can inter-work at the appropriate level within the architecture, they are analysed as a 'stack'. This stack is viewed as having hardware at its lowest level and applications software at its higher levels. At some level in the stack hierarchy, the infrastructure exists. This level as well as the content of the infrastructure may vary between sub-systems or stacks. This is why it is important to analyse the different stacks separately as well as in conjunction with the overall system architecture. From such an analysis, decisions of compatibility, cohesion and integration cost can be assessed. This is a necessary activity before a comprehensive implementation of groupware is undertaken.

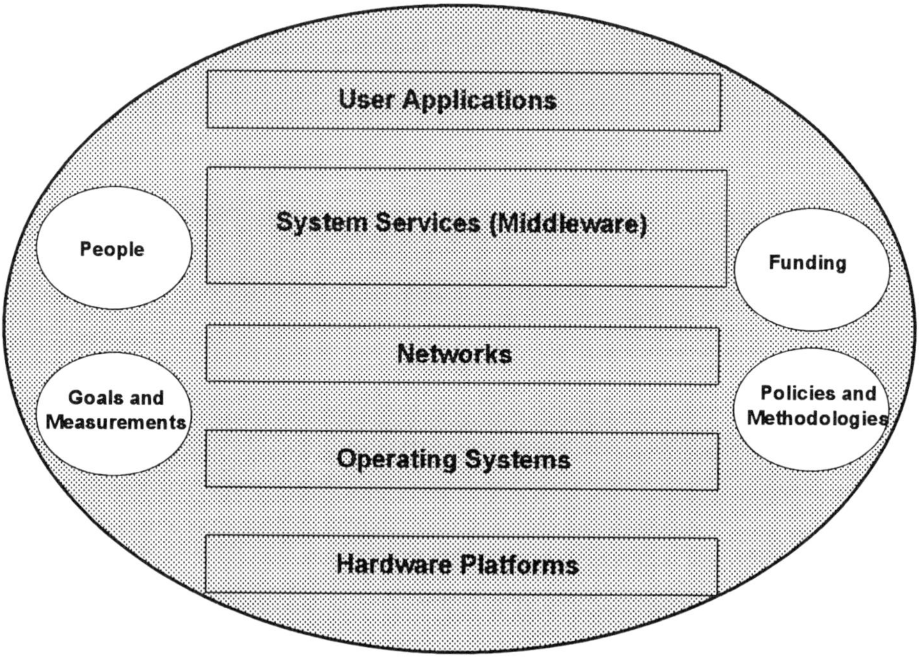

Figure 12.3 Components of an enterprise information architecture

The significance of these classifications to an organisation and its customers is that the infrastructure stacks to be used to deliver applications are moving from a mature architecture policy and standards environment to an environment where the standards are emerging or have still to be established. Many of the technologies associated with groupware, e.g., image compression, do not have clearly defined standards. This situation will cause added complications in systems development and necessitate additional standards related work. It will also increase the project risk.

This has important implications for the organisation. Risks and opportunities need to be managed by balancing the infrastructure design using mature infrastructure stacks (standards) whilst allowing for the introduction of emerging technology.

12.3.3 Linking business requirements to technical detail

The technical policies and standards should be structured so that the business strategy managers do not have to search through the technical detail in order to gain an appreciation of why there is a need for a common IT infrastructure. In addition, the document should also provide the link from business requirement to technical detail which is essential for the technicians to deliver flexible systems which meet the business requirements and conform to the common infrastructure.

The scope of the organisation's strategic IT requirements is such that no single set of technologies will adequately serve the entire spectrum of business needs. Within the common infrastructure are a number of technology sets, each with distinct characteristics, which, when linked with suitable interface technologies, can provide robust, flexible, cost-effective solutions.

In designing this infrastructure the balance which has to be achieved is between presenting an infrastructure which is a technologist's dream (or vision) and goes far beyond that which can be cost-justified by the business and the case of being too conservative in its anticipated use of developing technologies, causing the business to be unable to exploit the full benefits that could potentially be available from advances in technology.

12.4 What does the organisation require of IT?

This approach will enable an organisation to have a common technical approach which will provided a balance between cost effectiveness and business requirements within a consistent technical direction.

It should ensure that:

- all strategic systems are accessible through a common terminal system and across a common network
- multiple systems are operated and supported in a unified IT estate

- the skills built in the development of one strategic system can applied successfully to the development of others
- common items of data, such as name and address, are shared between strategy systems to improve the consistency of organisational data and reduce handling costs
- terminal dialogues are designed to ensure a consistent 'look and feel' between systems to allow flexibility in staff deployment and reduce training costs.

This type of strategy will provided an organisation with an infrastructure which will deliver enabled workgroup offices. This will be a unifying infrastructure supporting a cost effective development environment and providing the users with coherent applications.

12.5 The need for a unifying infrastructure

Although the components of the infrastructure are changing as new products are introduced into the market and the business units have more complex business requirements, there is still a need for an organisation to have a unifying infrastructure. Without one, continuous cost effective changes, will be difficult if not impossible to achieve.

There are many complexities in an infrastructure needed to support the size and diversity of a large groupware implementation. In order to control and plan an organisation's IT requirements, there is a need to understand these complexities and inter-relationships from a number of viewpoints. Each of these viewpoints are representative of a complete coherent structure. Some of the reasons why the architecture needs to be analysed from an number of viewpoints are now given. These include, to:-

- control the management of networked resources
- ensure appropriate ownership and security of data files
- validate and audit secure pathways
- understand the sequential flow of tasks through the system
- appreciate the changes and causes of change to data
- identify the topology of the network connections

- provide for and regulate the interfaces and transaction states for software execution
- identify the most suitable intercept points for technology refreshment
- encapsulate within the infrastructure the boundaries between developed and procured components and the resultant integration issues.

All IT systems have an architecture which either explicitly or implicitly describes how the hardware and software components are connected and inter-relate. However, unless there is a co-ordinated and centrally planned approach, the business applications will tend towards duplication, diversity and inflexibility. This is especially the case if tactical or expedient IT solutions are developed which do not fit into an agreed infrastructure strategy. Continued flexibility to shape the IT systems to meet the business requirements, within controlled cost parameters, can be achieved if the foundations or infrastructure has been so designed.

The approach of an organisation that wishes to introduce groupware enabled offices must be to establish a unifying infrastructure that is coherent, flexible and offers maximum opportunity for re-use. This approach will allow the organisation to be able to manage the diversity of technology; intercept new technology, where it makes business sense to do so. The Organisation should be able to get better value for money from its investment in IT and integrate groupware into the organisation effectively.

In order to achieve a unifying infrastructure which meets the needs of the organisation, is cost effective and flexible and provides the business units with a framework which enables them to plan a coherent long term groupware strategy, clearly defined technical policies and supporting standards need to be established.

12.5.1 Reasons for technical policies and standards

The link between the high level business policies and business drivers with the infrastructure components and products are the technical policies and supporting standards. The establishment and promulgation of organisational technical policies and standards not only provide a visible link between the business drivers and products through the product life cycle, but are also vital for a number of other reasons, namely to:

- clearly define established technical policies and standards for each infrastructure component and an indication of the emerging standards
- signpost the development of that component and therefore of the infrastructure
- allow infrastructure designers to define systems where the component parts inter-relate with each other with the minimum of integration
- help at the planning stage to ensure that there is a clearly defined migration path which will protect the investment in the infrastructure as well as providing the business benefit
- ensure reliability of product and cost minimisation
- aid rapid implementation by identifying proven standards and therefore products and indicates those areas which could cause delays because the standards have still to be established
- enable the end users to understand the level of complexity and (therefore cost) incorporating/integrating a product(s) into the infrastructure needed to satisfy a business driver.

Although these technical policies and supporting standards need to be clearly established, this has to take place within a framework where the organisation, business units and technical interests and requirements are balanced, for the benefit of all.

12.5.2 Ownership of policies and standards

Policies must be agreed, owned and managed centrally. A change control mechanism should be in place to manage the process. The standards needed to support the policies should also be owned by the organisation as an entity and not by a sub-set. A record of all standards should be centrally held. However, because the standards are used in the work situation, the custodianship and maintenance should be at the point of use by the practitioner. Change control would hold a profile of all standards and ensure there was no unnecessary duplications.

The organisation that generated the standards owns those standards and controls their release and maintenance. The owners and/or custodians of all standards adopted by an organisation should be known throughout that organisation.

A mechanism within each unit has to be in place to ensure that the standards are followed and adhered to. Ideally this is part of the quality initiative in so much that it becomes an integral part of the way in which people work. However, initially there is likely to be a need for standards audit and enforcement procedures.

The absence of policies and supporting standards makes control and quality measurements merely guesswork. The policies must be consistent and coherent, therefore they should be made centrally at the appropriate level, however, the standards, i.e., the specification of the products and services, should be held as close to the point of use as is feasible.

Technical policies will be developed to satisfy the following criteria:

- separating the design activity at the project level from the ratification process of the organisation's architecture policies (although in practice the teams would work closely together and act as a counter balance for each other)
- managing the generation of architecture policies within an agreed organisation-wide structure
- establishing an architecture policy adoption and ratification process
- reviewing policy gaps and placing priority ratings on each
- reviewing all existing and established architecture policies
- publishing in concise form agreed architecture policies
- identifying the types of standards required to support each architecture policy
- constructing a model to demonstrate to the business units the cost benefits of establishing co-ordinated common architecture policies and supporting standards

There is a need to clarify and/or establish standards to support the organisation's agreed technical policies. There are a number of actions involved which include:

- for adopted standards, identify and ratify the profile to be used by the organisation
- for all standards establish clear ownership
- for all standards establish change control management procedures
- recognise and minimise any duplication of standards for same purpose
- make standards freely available at the point of use
- technical policies are owned by the organisation
- the need to engineer high levels of flexibility to enable IT to respond smoothly and rapidly to changing business imperatives whilst equally ensuring that maximum opportunities can be gained from emerging technology
- the ever-increasing complexity of more advanced, rapidly changing technology distributed across greater areas
- the increasing reliance of the organisation upon IT together with the growing inter-dependence of IT with the individual.

Such reappraisal frequently signals the need for a radical shift in culture by both the IT practitioners and users alike; a need for greater mutual understanding and co-operation towards single business goals - the need for partnership.

12.6 The IT partnership

Devolution of IT responsibility whilst maintaining the organisation's objectives and establishing an effective unifying infrastructure requires collaborative partnership between business units and the central IT organisation to ensure that:-

- business units play a greater part in formulation of their future IT strategies
- organisational IT structures and procedures foster, rather than hinder, a spirit of openness and co-operation

- greater emphasis is placed upon producing well defined architectural principles, procedures practices and common architectural representation to which all parties are committed.

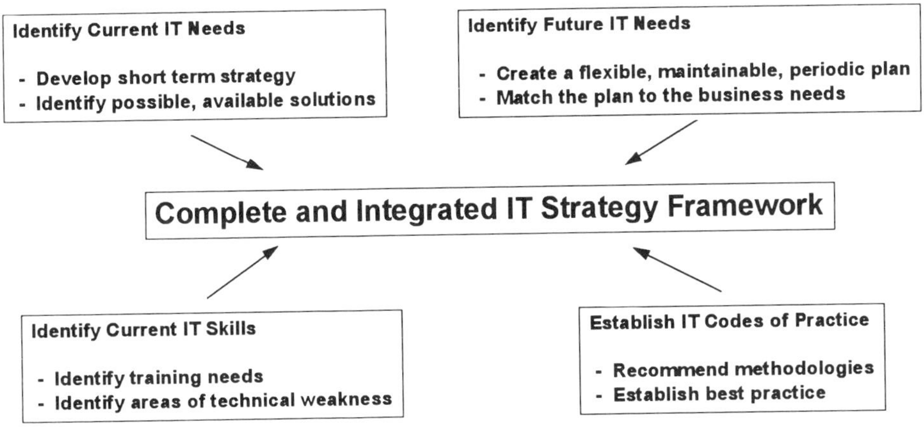

Figure 12.4 A technical architecture strategy

12.6 The need for an organisational IT authority

There is a need to maintain a central IT authority in support of a unifying infrastructure. However, whilst important from the technology viewpoint, there are other benefits in maintaining such an authority. For example, a single authority is well positioned to provide:

- the focus for ensuring that the unifying infrastructure satisfies the organisation, as well as specific business unit, objectives
- hence the medium through which the IT partnership between the organisation, the business units and the supplier(s) can be enabled.

12.6.1 Product life cycle

Those organisations which develop clearly established technical policies and standards use them to manage the product life cycle. Polices and standards are used to provide the mechanism to control the specification of any products within the procurement process. This is part of a cycle or series of linked events that include:

- identification of business drivers (the organisation and business units)

- alignment process
- identify required infrastructure
- establish the technical policies required to support the infrastructure
- document the standards required to support the technical policies
- acquisition/development of products against the agreed standards
- integration tasks
- delivery and end-user sign off
- maintenance commitment
- product withdrawal.

Each of these entities has a 'visible deliverable' which can be used to control and monitor the various processes.

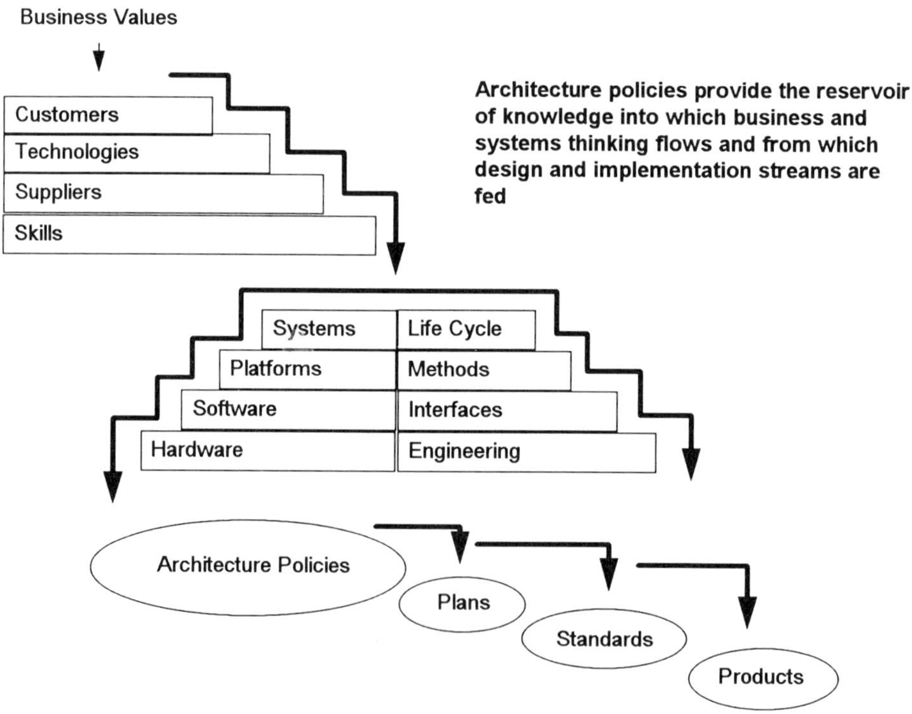

Figure 12.5 Relationship between product mix and architecture policies

12.6.2 Presentation of policies and standards

This approach enables the presentation of policies and standards in a way in which it:

- displays and links business drivers, architecture policies, supporting standards, products and integration tasks
- demonstrates the impact that business drivers (the organisation and business units) have on existing infrastructure policies
- explains the relationships and inter-dependencies between business drivers, supporting standards, products and integration tasks
- allows management to display 'impact analysis' which enables them to visibly trade off requirements against a finite resource base
- illustrates the evolving infrastructure deliverables within the context of the business driven IT environment, thereby increasing the understanding and awareness of infrastructure
- provides a public relations interface needed to provide both information and the basis for a forum
- provides management information in a way that could help encourage a culture of shared values where those responsible for implementing can understand the justification and rationale underlying management decisions.

12.7 Relationship between business drivers, technical policies and standards

There are well established links and relationships between business drivers, technical policies, standards and work activities.

12.7.1 Technical policies and business drivers

Technical policies support decisions made at the technical system option stage of a project such as the 'best fit' within an overall product operating regime, to satisfy the business drivers and user requirements.

12.7.2 Technical policies and standards

The standards are specifications for authorised interfaces, procedures, products and services needed to support approved technical policies.

12.7.3 Standards, products and work activities

The process of developing products to a set of standards (specifications) or matching existing products against a set of specification creates work activities or projects.

12.8 Scope of framework

The framework is designed to enable optimisation of a unifying infrastructure which affords maximum benefit to the business units whilst equally meeting overall organisational objectives.

There will be certain instances where a particular business unit requirement can more adequately be provided through IT which is not necessarily part of such an infrastructure. In such cases, conformity to the framework will not constitute a pre-condition provided that the IT in question will, where appropriate, interface with such an infrastructure. A useful analogy is that of connecting third party devices to the public telephone network.

Applications fall into this category in as much as they are likely to be unique to a Business Unit and, whilst not being a part of the infrastructure, they will probably need to interface to the unifying infrastructure.

Chapter 13. The new way of computing: infrastructure and the groupware solution

The groupware applications need to be supported by an appropriate infrastructure. This infrastructure will have to be common across the whole of the organisation and in many cases be able to link in with suppliers' and customers' infrastructure. For most organisations this level of integrated infrastructure does not exist To get to this level will require considerable investment in the new wave of developments.

The trend towards a new IT infrastructure has many names, and will no doubt continue to acquire even more names as the marketing people try to distinguish their product from the offerings of their competitors. As far as the end-user organisation is concerned this new infrastructure will have to contain the set of information technologies that the organisation has determined to be relevant and requisite to meet the business objectives.

13.1 The new way of computing

AT&T uses the phrase "the new way of computing", which has the advantage that the intuitive obvious meaning is correct. We also refer to workgroup enabling architecture which should be a formal specification of the policies and technical standards which the organisation will use when introducing groupware into the organisation. These policies must determine how the infrastructure will be organised and the applications executed.

The new way of computing in the late 1990s and early 21st century will be characterised by a focus on user effectiveness. As we have explained, this will involve the empowerment of individuals and small groups into productive work groups. One of their main enabling tools will be the high-performance workstations with organised access to enterprise computing resources. These will include data sources and access to the processes and people which are needed to be productive. The emphasis will be increasingly on being productive.

13.2 Access to data

This access to data sources and processes will require peer-to-peer networking, mapped to the increase of cross-functional communication at the personal level. This will involve cooperative processing with single applications deployed across multiple systems, often of different sizes and types.

In order to empower the user, the workstation will have to support multiple information forms, i.e., data, graphics, image, voice. This will put heavy demands onto the infrastructure, especially the message carrying components. The component of the infrastructure which is involved in the message carrying is known as the middleware. This is the system services between the operating system and the application that have the effect of rendering the operating system and hardware platform transparent to the developer and the end user. It is essential that this aspect of the infrastructure is robust since it will be needed when new applications are added.

13.3 Most organisations carry a legacy

For organisations considering the implementation of workgroup applications using an enhanced infrastructure, there will be increasing need to develop a migration policy from the old infrastructure to the new. The migration policy should set out to protect the everyday business interests by planning the introduction of the new systems to cause the minimum of disruption and the maximum of business benefit.

To support the new way of computing, it becomes readily apparent that the planning and execution of the transition from the existing architecture to new architecture is critical.

Most large organisations from all sectors now have complex, multi-vendor computing strategies which have not been planned as a total entity for the organisation. They are often characterised by non-integrated islands of automation and huge legacy software investment which is not the infrastructure needed to support a groupware implementation. The situation is often complicated by the existence of professional IT staff who are determined to support and defend their island of information and who are able to come up with many reasons why it cannot or should not be integrated into a corporate common infrastructure. In these types of situations many issues other than 'what is best for the business' have to be addressed This is why start up companies can steal a march on the established companies by introducing new infrastructure which will support new productive ways of working. Many of the most effective proponents of groupware are organisations which do not have a legacy of different systems and conflicting IT staff.

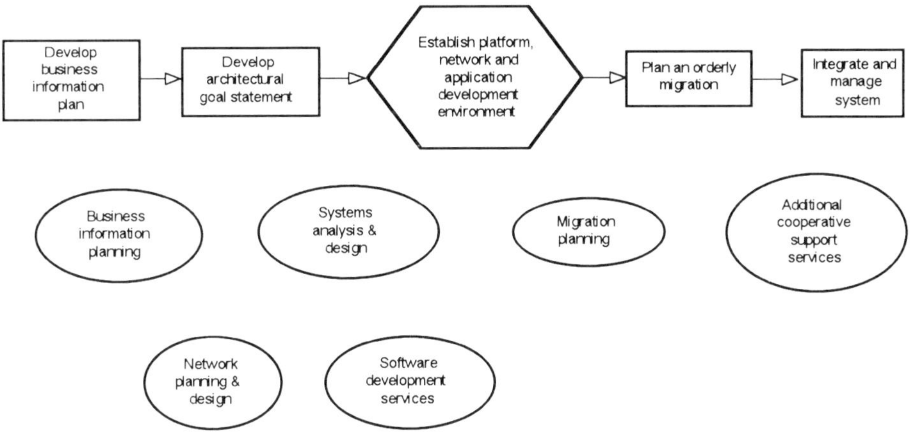

Figure 13.1 The transition to open cooperative computing

Organisations with systems and staff that are out of date or at least out of place in the context of the 21st century will have to undertake an exercise to retrain the whole of their staff or at least those who are capable of being retrained. The IT staff are in an similar situation to the white collar workers they are there to support - the main difference is that they do not understand the business and have technical skills that are out of date. The ones with the most difficulty are those who still think that networked personal computers and client-server architecture can not deal with a core system of a large company.

13.4 Retraining for a new culture

This retraining exercise will often involve rebuilding a whole culture. For many of the IT staff this will mean a shift away from the mainframe glass house mentality, to one that supports the new way of computing. This is not be an easy task and increasingly large organisations are releasing IT staff or market testing the problem by using facilities management. This however, will create other problems.

Although there are many cries by respected senior staff that it is not possible to make these moves all at once it does not equate with the voice from the market. Change is happening and the question is do you want to be part of it or do you want to watch it from a safe distance as a non-active observer.

Business and architectural change are happening and will continue to happen.

13.5 The impetus for change

There are an number of forces of change in an industry-wide shift to new ways of computing. These include:

- down costing forced by intense global competition pressures on costs now that mainframes are widely understood to have lost combativeness and functional superiority
- restructuring of the enterprise business architecture with the focus on empowering the individuals and small work groups and the goal of enhancing enterprise responsiveness
- the acceptance and maturity of the open systems movement with widespread vendor commitment to technologies that permit application portability, systems interoperability and cross-vendor manageability.

13.6 The forces against change

At the same time, two negative forces are at work to slow down the shift - both are predicable with any significant innovations. The first is the information lag associated with a complex new technology.

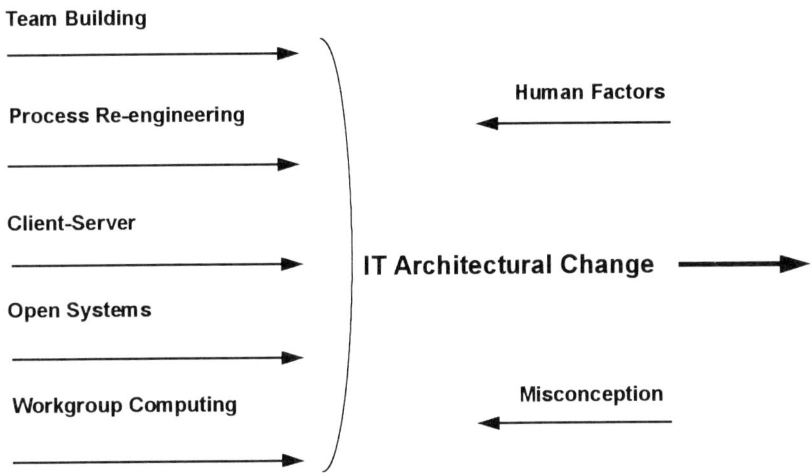

Figure 13.2 The vectors of change

The engineers who built understand it, but do not necessarily understand its impact. Customers do not understand it and have to interpret its potential impact from superficial data - sales and promotional material. This tends to produce conservative interpretations, sprinkled here and there with over optimism. The sales forces in the middle have little more knowledge about the new technology than the customer they are trying to inform.

The information lag plays right into the second negative force: human resistance to change. IT users are particularly prone to clinging to old concepts, since the stakes are so high. "This may not be new but we know it works".

13.6.1 Resistance to change has to be overwhelmed

Nevertheless, resistance to change is being overwhelmed by the three positive forces. Downcosting provides a particularly powerful motivator for change in the lean years. Successful downcosting initiatives have delivered anywhere from 20 per cent to 50 per cent reductions in total information systems expenditure.

Changes in business architecture forced the use of distributed minicomputers in the 1970s and of personal computers in the 1980s, both over central IT authority opposition. This will bring unrelenting pressure on the IT community in the 1990s until the IT architecture maps to the business architecture and is lean, cost-effective and focused on empowerment This will require change.

Finally acceptance of open systems has rightly become the new orthodoxy raising the risk for IT professionals who are proponents of vendor lock-in.

13.7 Groupware model of change

We offer a simple model that shows the interaction between groupware business architecture and groupware IT architecture. The model starts with the business drivers, a set of reality that includes legal, geographical, human, competitive and technological opportunities and constraints that bear on how the organisation must operate to succeed. The business architecture stems from the business drivers and includes specific products and services that the organisation will market, talent pools it will recruit and organise, policies it will develop to govern corporate behaviour and value systems it will cultivate over time.

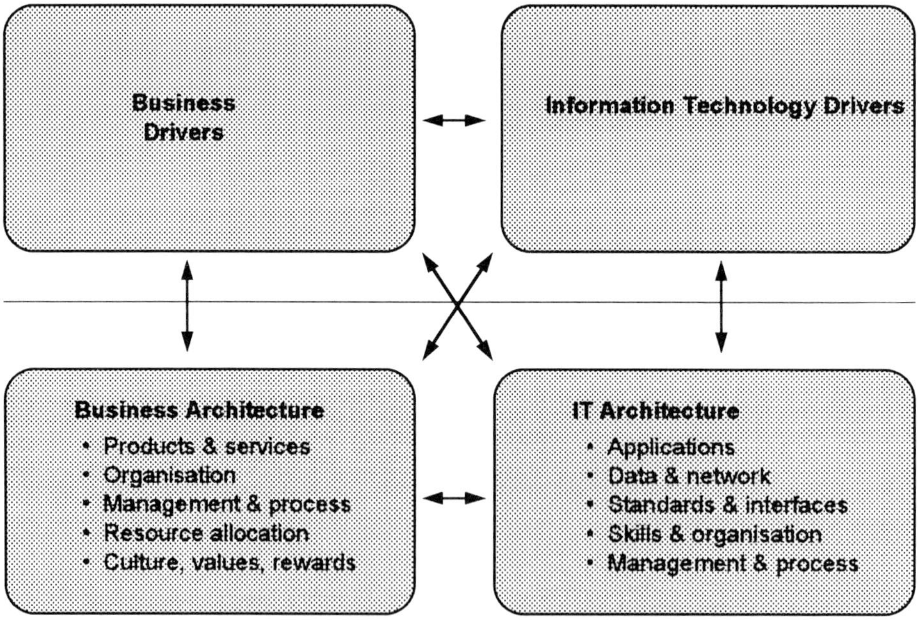

Figure 13.3 The Groupware model of change

The business drivers have parallel IT drivers - the subset of available IT technology relevant to a specific organisation. For example, a single sourced insurance company with one office is unlikely to find distributed database or distributed transaction processing technology relevant. Those same technologies will be highly relevant to an insurance company that distributes globally from multiple offices and therefore will be part of its IT drivers. The IT architecture derives from the IT drivers and includes the human resources, methodologies, computer platforms and products, IT polices and standards as well as the metrics of how the IT will operate to support the organisation.

Changes in the business drivers will cause changes in the derived business architecture, in the IT drivers and in the derived IT architecture. In those cases where the formal IT organisation fails to adjust to changes to the business drivers, the business managers must and will find ways to bypass the IT organisation. The business is there to service the customer, not the whims of the IT department.

13.8 Business managers have acted unilaterally before

In the 1970s, business units brought in mini computers because of the slow response of the central IT department. In the 1980s, the personal computer was the pressure valve. Conversely changes in available IT technology can and will provide opportunities for new business initiatives

In order to capitalise on these IT breakthroughs and enable new business initiatives organisations will continue to push real authority down to business managers. Since IT strategy is increasingly central to business unit success (and business unit managers know it) the newly empowered managers will insist on influencing IT strategy.

Multiple business units, each with a strong chief executive will create multiple IT strategies often involving multiple vendors. Organisational integration will therefore require the ability to port and interoperate infrastructure applications across multiple platforms and to communicate across all systems on a peer-to-peer basis. These are key capabilities of the new IT master platforms, but are noticeably lacking in traditional architectures.

13.9 Standards

Successful enterprises will establish strong links to their business partners in both directions of the supply chain. This will have a number of effects:

- even when a large organisation has constrained itself to one computer vendor and one computer architecture external links will create multi vendor integration
- the market will force all computer company vendors to support open standards, then open standards will become the most likely mechanism for inter-enterprise exchanges. Adopted internally open standards minimise the number of technologies that have to be supported.

13.10 Open systems technology

The accelerating movement towards open systems is observable and unmistakable, The decision to move to open systems did not originate in IT but was forced on IT by the business managers.

There are a number of roles and goals of open systems:

- open means permitting vendor independence and enabling multi-vendor integration. The attraction is low cost, lower risk and increased flexibility (to enable a wide range of technologies to be integrated)
- open also means permitting application portability, systems interoperability and enterprise wide systems manageable in a multi vendor situation
- for the end user it is open that means that he can buy it without being hassled by IT compatibility
- all the user wants is low cost, ease of use, minimal retaining over time, rich functionality and access to the enterprise computing assets.

13.10.1 Need to demonstrate speed

Survivors in the late 1990s and early 21st century will have to demonstrate speed - the ability to manage speed. Speed in the development of new products and services, in manufacturing, in delivery and above all in recognising changes in market demands or technologies and reaching decisions to respond.. To support this speed-up organisations will include in their new way of computing which will have to respond with speed.

The main technologies which are required include:

- enterprise electronic mail that can handle compound documents
- binary large objects (BLOB) support in databases, primarily on non volatile objects in relational databases
- workflow management systems to administer the decision process and ensure the delivery of decisions-support data and documentation
- point-of-transactions, palm-top devices and wireless communications to eliminate any delay in acquiring data
- advanced work stations with very high MIPS rates and high performance graphics for computer
- scaleability in a single architecture from desktop to mainframe now delivered by AT&T, DEC and HP will become common attributes from successful vendors
- distributed databases and transactions will map naturally to the increasingly global nature of large companies and to increase joint activities between companies.
- open standards to ensure ease of integration
- high speed development environment must be in place to deal with the need to respond quickly to a changing market.

13.11 Fitting in with the groupware pyramid principle

In this section we have described how to set about designing the appropriate architecture to support a groupware implementation. The pyramid shown in figure 13.4 shows the specific technologies involved in this stage.

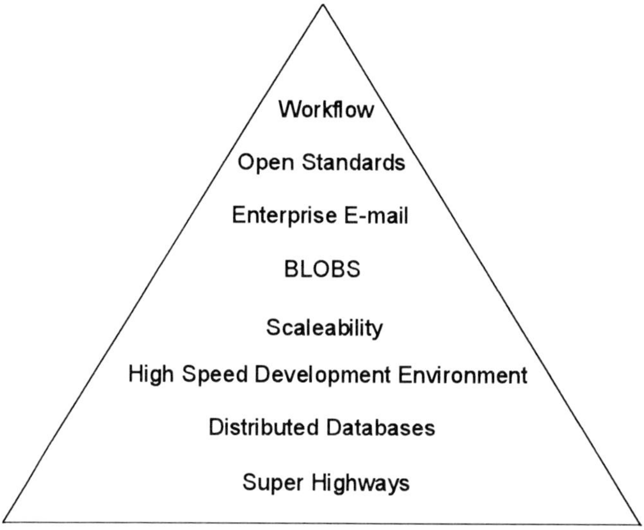

Figure 13.4 An alternative pyramid for groupware infrastructure

Figure 13.5 shows the general path in the groupware pyramid which this stage must follow. If all the generic stages are complete, an IT infrastructure appropriate for a groupware solution should be produced.

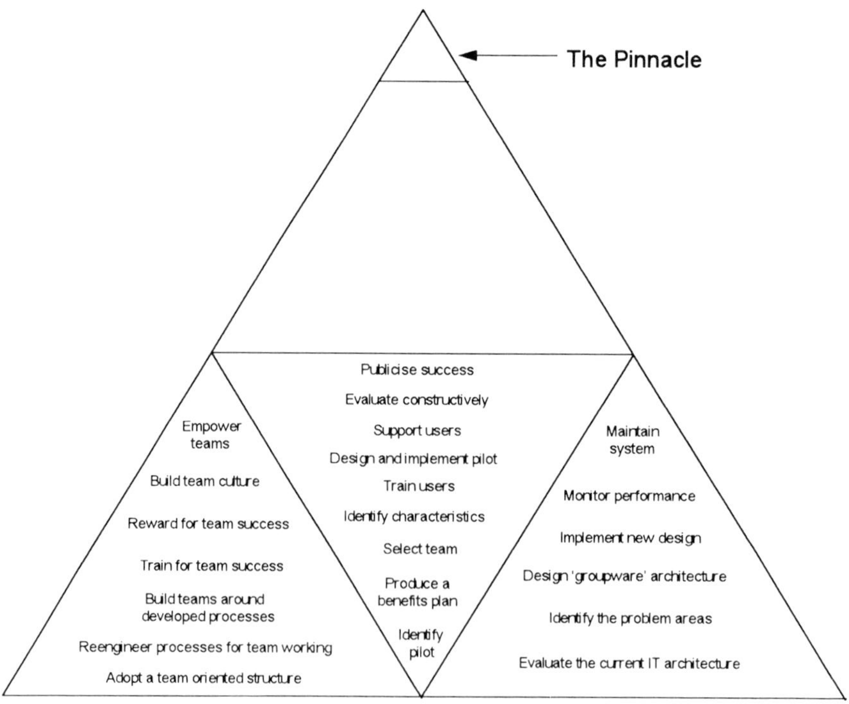

Figure 13.5 The third block is in place

Section VI. The risks and benefits of groupware

Chapter 14. Growing big

The benefits that can be obtained from a successful groupware implementation are many and varied but it is also important to note that there a number of potential risks lurking around most corners. These risks will be minimised if groupware is implemented with care, following a pre-defined methodology such as the Groupware Pyramid Principle presented throughout this book.

Measuring and documenting the benefits realised from a groupware project is not a simple task because many of them are intangible and contribute to business success in a way that cannot have an accurate monetary value put on it. The benefits obtained from the pilot system must be measured and reported in order to provide the justification for expansion into other areas of the organisation.

14.1 Post pilot implementation

Once the pilot project has been completed, hopefully successfully and with much publicity, the benefits need to be quantified so that adequate justification can be made for an expansion into other areas of the business. This process will be made easier if a business plan was laid out before the pilot implementation. If this is the case, the actual benefits obtained can be compared with the anticipated benefits that provided the justification for the pilot system in the first instance.

If the pilot is a success and the benefits obtained can be used to justify further expansion, other areas of the business which could benefit substantially from groupware need to be identified. Initially, as groupware is still in the fertilisation stages within an organisation, each new project must aim to deliver the same quick hits as the pilot system. This will ensure that groupware grows the necessary roots to be implemented across the breadth of the organisation.

Each implementation should be carefully planned with the same steps being taken as with the pilot project. Work group characteristics should be identified and it is important to remember that each work group will have different needs which may require the use of alternative groupware products or even a different implementation approach. Training is still essential and complacency must not be allowed to set in if groupware implementations become increasingly successful within the company. Most importantly, the success of the additional projects must be celebrated so that eventually the whole organisation wants to be given the facilities that groupware provides and true company wide buy-in is achieved.

Identifying and reporting the benefits of the pilot system provides the ground work for the last stage of the groupware pyramid principle to be put in place. The benefits will provide justification for further projects which if successful will again provide justification for further expansion. This stage in the methodology is iterative:

- define additional areas of the business where groupware would provide significant gains
- identify characteristics
- design system
- generate benefits plan
- implement system
- train and educate
- measure success
- justify further projects

This cycle is continued until company wide buy-in has been achieved at which point the organisation will have reached the pinnacle of the pyramid. This will be the stage at which the organisation has a total information sharing culture, a communications system which operates without regard to time and place, a team working and collaborative culture, a network management structure with empowered teams and a customer facing, process oriented business.

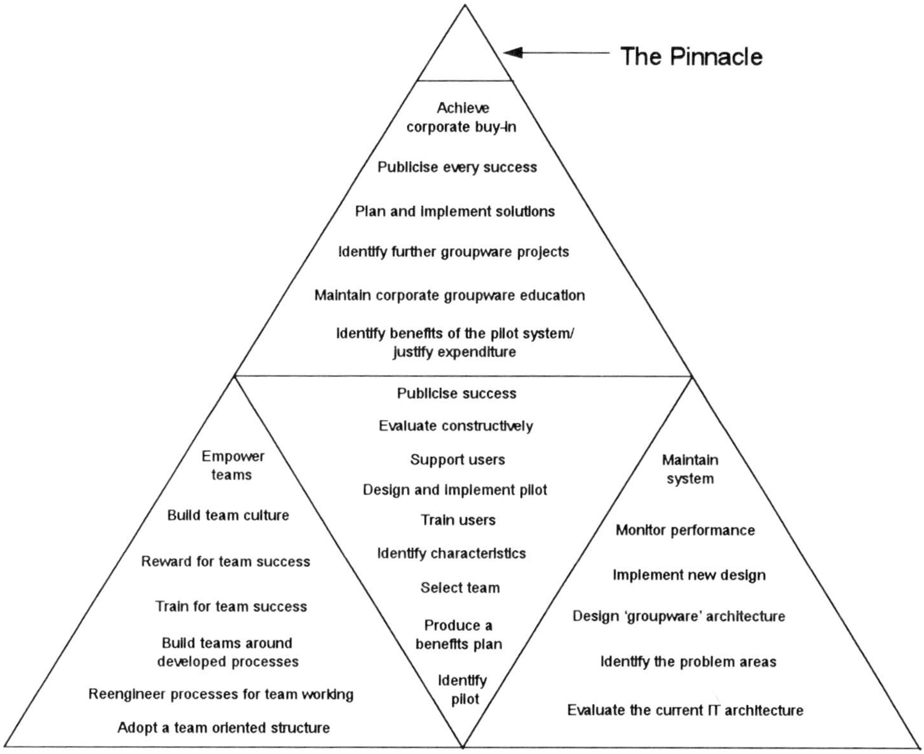

Figure 14.1 Reaching the pinnacle

Chapter 15. Avoiding the risks

There are a number of potential pitfalls associated with a groupware implementation because the technology is so revolutionary in its impact. Most of these risks are obvious and can be easily avoided with detailed planning and adherence to a defined implementation methodology.

The main risks that face a groupware project stem from one of three areas:

- people problems
- architecture problems
- software problems

15.1 People problems

In many IT projects, the implementation team spend 80 per cent of their time worrying about the technology and only 20 per cent on people issues. The result is that 80 per cent of failures are due to people problems and only 20 per cent to technology problems - even these are generally attributed to human error. The lesson to be learnt here is that the users are equally as important as the technology. They are the ones who will be exploiting the system and however good and innovative the technology, 'if the users don't use it, it's not worth having'.

People issues are especially important in the move to groupware because of the impact that the technology will have on the environment and working procedures. Its introduction will attempt to change these for the better but it is important to realise that change can be inspiring but can also be demoralising and disruptive. Care must be taken to ensure that the change is inspiring and this means involving the user population and providing them with education and support programmes.

Some of the potential people problems that may be encountered during a groupware implementation are:

- Some people may not work well in a team environment - overcome by:
  - ~ promoting the success of team working prior to implementation
  - ~ giving the appropriate training in interpersonal and team building skills
  - ~ by building teams of employees who work well together
  - ~ by providing the team with work which fulfils the five criteria outlined in section 8.4.
- Employees may be reluctant to share their business knowledge - knowledge is sometimes regarded as power, especially the higher up a company you go. Employees may feel that if they divulge their knowledge they may lose their property of being indispensable. Hsu and Lockwood [*1993*] note that "often people perceive their value to a company as their expertise, and if they share that expertise, they've lost their value. But frequently it turns out to be the other way around - their co-workers find out just how valuable they are to the company". This is the point that must be promoted - that employees are likely to progress further if people discover what they know.
- Former middle managers may not adapt well to working in a team at the same level as those that used to work under them - overcome by:
  - ~ giving the previous middle managers roles within the team such as consultant, advisor or trainer
  - ~ using their management experience in the transformation to a team structure.
- The increased use of electronic communication and meeting systems may isolate some teams or individuals - using electronic communication techniques reduces the amount of face-to-face interaction between employees; those involved in teleworking may have no face-to-face interaction at all. This is a culture shock which must be recognised and dealt with. The benefits of electronic communication are obvious but employees will still demand the

social aspect that communicating face-to-face provides for them. One solution to this is to hold frequent team or department meetings where socialising is promoted and a greater sense of 'groupness' can be established.

- Electronic communications can be disruptive and cause ill feeling - although true anonymity is not provided by e-mail, communication is not face-to-face and it is therefore easier to express feelings and say certain things. If e-mail is primarily used to convey negative feelings and opinions, it can be incredibly disruptive and demoralising for certain individuals. This may lead to them not reading their messages and an escalation of this can lead to a communications collapse. There is no obvious solution for this problem apart from providing other means for workers to express their feelings and promoting an open working environment where individuals are trained in the art of giving and receiving constructive criticism.

15.2 Architecture problems

Some implementation failures can be attributed to technology problems and in a groupware project, the underlying IT infrastructure forms a vital component. Some of the more common problems in this area are given below:

- The network is unreliable - the use of groupware requires the availability of a reliable and efficient network to facilitate the communication and collaboration that the software promotes. If the necessary network services are not available or the communication facilities are unreliable, users will become frustrated and begin to underuse the features of the software. This can be overcome by ensuring that an adequate and scaleable network infrastructure is already in place prior to any groupware implementation. Scaleability is important - as the groupware bug catches on, more communications will be passed via the network and it will undoubtedly have to be expanded to cover other areas of the business or to allow the passing of more sophisticated multi-media data.
- Corporate data memory is inadequate - many groupware implementations will be based around a corporate database which

acts as the 'organisational memory'. This database is likely to be huge as more forms of data are stored from an increasing number of sources. The database management system which is chosen to handle this memory bank must therefore be capable of holding vast amounts of data, must be scaleable and must support a wide range of data types.

- PC or workstation base is inefficient - groupware software is extremely complex and is becoming increasingly so. This means that to run effectively, powerful PCs or workstations are required with graphical user interfaces and perhaps multi-media capabilities. Running groupware on out-of-date machines will cause frustration to the users who will spent a lot of time waiting for things to happen. This will also be of detriment to the impression that is created of groupware within the organisation. To prevent this occurrence, powerful, flexible and upgradeable PCs and workstations should be used with multi-media facilities if appropriate.

15.3 Software problems

In addition to technology problems, the software used or written for the implementation may be the cause of failure. Some potential software problems are given below:

- Software is not appropriate for the team or the organisation as a whole - we stressed in an earlier section of the book the importance of analysing groups and the processes they carry out. This analysis should be performed at the group level but should never be performed on an entity greater than a department. The needs of teams and departments will vary so much that it is unlikely a single groupware product will be appropriate company wide - there is no panacea where groupware is concerned. The groupware products should be chosen to complement the group. Buying a groupware product and then forming work patterns and processes to suit this will only end in disappointing results. Processes must be identified along with the work group's characteristics so that a product can be chosen to support the particular aspects of the individual teams. The pilot project should also be used to ensure that the chosen products are appropriate.

- The developed groupware systems are unreliable and ineffective - most groupware products provide the means to develop specialised systems so that a degree of tailoring is possible throughout the organisation. These products usually support rapid systems development techniques by providing object-oriented development environments along with code generators and object libraries. It is very tempting to use these facilities to produce a quick and dirty working system for the pilot and merely extend this for the full roll out. Developing rapid systems is appropriate for the pilot but when it comes to the full implementation, rapid development techniques should be used with caution and only in situations where experienced developers are writing the system to an agreed and detailed specification and design. Presenting users with software which is unreliable, inefficient and unpredictable will cause them much distress and only add to the problems of coping with change.
- The developed system does not complement the business processes or the team's way of working - an integral part of moving to groupware is an analysis of the business processes. This serves a number of purposes: it allows the processes to be reengineered to eradicate inefficiencies, allows complementary and appropriate software products to be chosen and provides a means by which systems can be specified. If this analysis is performed, developing groupware software to complement business processes should be a relatively simple affair.

15.4 Other potential risks

Other risks which should be considered and planned for include:

- Information and communication overload - the communication and information sharing facilities that groupware provides may bring the problem of information and communication overload. Before the implementation, employees, managers and executives may have found that they did not have enough of the right information to perform their function. The introduction of groupware may reverse this situation to the extent where users cannot cope with the shear abundance of information they are receiving. This situation can be avoided by providing guidelines suggesting when it is and isn't appropriate to use electronic communications (there is nothing worse than arriving at work in the morning and spending until lunch time just reading your mail messages) and when priorities should and shouldn't be attached. Careful design of the organisational memory and the subsets of data distributed to the users will also prevent the dispatch and availability of unnecessary data.

- Greater reliance on computer skilled staff - given the complexity of groupware products and their rapid introduction into the business world, the number of groupware literate employees will be in short supply in the next few years. This will lead to organisations placing greater reliance on such employees. To overcome this problem, organisations will have to ensure that adequate training is provided to those users making the transition to groupware and for any new joiners entering a groupware environment for the first time. We talked about the training that users should receive in section 9.2.
- Greater reliance on computer systems - most organisations already rely heavily on their computer systems on a day-to-day basis and a serious computer breakdown would spell disaster. The introduction of groupware will make organisations place even greater reliance on their computer systems with more information stored electronically and a greater percentage of communications conducted via electronic means. Employing modern and proven technology, implemented by experts will help to reduce the frequency of systems collapse.
- Invasion of privacy - even in a total information sharing environment, there will always be some information that must remain of a personal and private nature. Users may be concerned that such information will lose its confidentiality during the move to groupware. They must be convinced otherwise, perhaps by producing a security document detailing how this will be achieved.

Chapter 16. The benefits of groupware

Groupware promises to achieve a wide range of benefits and to reverse the historical trend of IT investments realising few or no productivity gains. Large groupware implementations are still quite few and far between but those reported on have been tremendous successes.

Citibank Mortgage, part of Citibank UK, implemented a workflow automation system to combat the problem of files not being available 35 per cent of the time because they were located elsewhere. The benefits of this implementation have been a productivity improvement of 50 per cent (compared to a expected 10 per cent), a much faster service to customers, better management control and a saving in office space.

At the start of 1993, Colorgraphic, a design and printing firm, installed a video conferencing system to enable them to communicate effectively with their customers in Germany, Belgium and the Netherlands. This allows them to meet 'face-to-face' with their clients and to demonstrate the look and feel of products which they formally had to send by post at a cost of £80. The system also allows drawings to be shown on screen and amended in real-time. The main drawback of the system is the quality of the pictures but this will improve with advances in technology and communications facilities. Colorgraphic estimates that it has saved £12,500 in time, travel and courier costs in its first year with its four £5000 trial units. Chief Executive Mike Hunter enthuses, "It's excellent, I'm very impressed".

Met Life, one of the largest insurance organisations in the United States, implemented groupware to keep track of speeches written for senior officers, to keep tabs on competitive information, to track major news items and to help compile internal reports. This has brought them many benefits by helping them manage and share information more easily.

National Provident Institution introduced groupware technology to manage the flow of information involved in the process of dealing with insurance claims. The implementation brought many benefits to this previously manual activity including: improved customer service, faster response to queries and fewer paper-bound clerical procedures.

Barclays Registrars implemented a groupware solution which enabled them to generate more than four times as many customer letters a week with 98 per cent turned around in less than 48 hours, occupy one third of the previous office space and redeploy 27 surplus staff.

Polymer Laboratories implemented a groupware solution to help co-ordinate the activities of their sales and service forces and the product development teams which were spread over four different sites. The benefits of the system were reported as being: improved flow of information around the company, a significant reduction in paperwork, the ability to present a united face to its customers and a low cost global network [*Bartram and Youett 1993*].

16.1 Justifying a groupware project

Groupware is a new technology which is still not widely understood within the IT and business communities. As with other emerging technologies such as client server, object-orientation and truly open systems, justifying an investment in groupware and subsequently measuring the benefits is extremely difficult. This is the case for many of today's IT investments because of the complex technology being implemented and the demand for an adequate return on investment.

16.1.1 Traditional justification and evaluation techniques

Traditional techniques which have been used to justify IT investments over the past thirty years or so are no longer adequate when considering some of today's new and advanced concepts. This is mainly due to the fact that today's technology offers a lot more than the conventional business benefits of increased productivity and reduced costs. Other reasons for the inadequacy of justification techniques such as Discounted Cashflow and Return on Investment are:

- the increasing complexity and sophistication of IT systems which frequently involves lengthy implementation cycles
- the decision to implement strategic IT systems is being made by more senior managers within an organisation - in a recent survey, over 50 per cent of the decisions to implement client/server technologies within the Fortune 1000 firms were made at the corporate level
- the fact that managers now demand more linkage between their strategic business objectives and the IT investments
- the history of IT investments realising small and insignificant benefits.

16.2 Advanced justification and evaluation techniques

Fortunately, there are many innovative methods being used by progressive firms to justify and measure the benefits obtained from large IT investments. These methods can be used to assist in the justification of a pilot project, to measure the benefits of the pilot and to further justify expansion of the implementation. More importantly, they can provide enormous help in developing a benefits plan prior to a groupware pilot so that justifiable benefits can be reported at the end. These new justification approaches can be split into two categories: cost reduction and strategic approaches. All of the following techniques are appropriate to a groupware project and have been adapted for this purpose.

16.2.1 Cost reduction approaches

Work value analyses

This approach is justified upon a recognition that white collar workers routinely perform activities of different intrinsic value to the organisation, and that one of the primary benefits of groupware is its ability to restructure work patterns. Thus the benefits of groupware include not only increased efficiency (doing the same work faster and more cost effectively) but also increased effectiveness (performing higher value work on processes which have been redesigned for the work group scenario).

Using this approach requires that an initial work value analysis of the organisation be performed. This will evaluate the current efficiency of processes and the value of the work being carried out by employees. The necessary step of analysing business processes prior to a groupware implementation provides an opportunity to perform such a study and the results will provide a sound basis against which to evaluate the benefits of the subsequent implementation

This approach has been successfully applied at General Motors over the recent past and a report focusing on white collar work at five major US corporations claimed that many organisations can reduce the office payroll by 15 per cent if they recalibrate their staffing mix and increase the intellectual specialisation of their work force. Groupware provides the opportunity to do exactly that - empower teams.

Cost of quality

The total resources of an organisation can always be divided into 'value added' activities or 'cost of quality' activities. Companies strive to reduce the cost of quality activities whilst allowing their work force to concentrate on adding value to clients through producing higher quality goods or providing better customer service. Cost of quality activities mainly involve the costs associated with failure, whether this be in the production or design of a product or in the distribution of a service. By allowing effective communication and collaboration between employees and by facilitating the production of an organisational memory and information sharing culture, groupware effectively reduces the cost of quality activities involved in communicating, cooperating and using information. It allows employees to concentrate on value added activities by providing them with work procedures suited to a team environment, the necessary information to perform their function and the tools that they require.

Many experts believe that by using the management concepts highlighted in this book (flatter, network management structure and empowered teams) and by supporting the users with a rich set of groupware tools, organisations can direct up to 95 per cent of their resources into value added activities. Reducing the cost of quality and adding to the value of the organisation provides a powerful means of justifying an investment. Measuring the results can also lead to significant benefits being identified. It has been said that in many companies, management can make more profits by cutting poor quality costs in half than by doubling sales or halving the work force. This can be accomplished without hiring one new person, building one new building or discovering one more customer. There is money lying all around an organisation - all you need to do is go out find it, pick it up and put it back in the bank.

16.2.2 Strategic approaches

Option value

Investment in IT is sometimes justified by highlighting the options that the new technology will provide for the future. IT can provide an organisation with the opportunity to gain a competitive edge in the future by making them more flexible, adaptable and responsive to change. Groupware does just this. The implementation of groupware gives the organisation a number of possibilities in the way that business processes are performed and the way that the company is structured. Groupware also makes a company more responsive to changes in the market because teams and processes can be established on a 'need' basis.

This approach is concerned with asking the questions - 'What opportunities will groupware provide us with in the future?'. 'How can we use this technology to give ourselves a leading edge?'.

Drawing a decision tree may help in this process, i.e., if we take step A, what opportunities will that give us in the future? By doing this, it will become obvious that a groupware solution along with the associated restructuring and redesign, will provide for endless opportunities in the future. Most experts in this area agree that identifying and evaluating the potential impact of strategic options is frequently the most valuable part of an IT investment.

Technical importance

Groupware provides the stimulus for an organisation to move out of a sluggish period and focus on the future by making a fresh start. Many organisations have found that groupware provides the means for them to move forward and that without the technical innovation they would have continued to stagnate. When groupware is implemented for this purpose - providing the stimulus for change - immediate and tangible benefits may be negligible. The implementation will still prove invaluable as it becomes the enabler for future, more complex and desirable projects to be undertaken. Identifying these projects will help to justify the investment and by proving that such projects are possible once the technology is in place, a significant benefit has been identified.

Competitive advantage

Groupware is new, leading edge technology and is currently being used by organisations to gain a competitive edge. It can be used to make organisations more flexible, more efficient and it allows them to provide improved customer service. Identifying the competitive advantages that groupware can provide for an organisation gives a sound base against which to measure the benefits. Typical competitive advantages stemming from groupware include:

- increased access to business information, especially customer information
- providing more information for customers and suppliers
- providing an improved customer service
- reducing costs and improving productivity
- reducing the time to design and deliver a new product or service
- creating a more enthusiastic, motivated and educated work force.

16.2.3 Summary

Today, IT investments are becoming more costly, more risky and have the potential of imposing significant changes on an organisation. This requires that the justification techniques used have to recognise this fact and go beyond identifying the traditional business benefits of improved productivity and reduced costs. They must be capable of demonstrating the 'soft' strategic benefits that will be realised as well as the 'hard' business benefits that are demanded by all investments, not just in IT. It is important to draw the distinction between hard and soft benefits because groupware's added value comes in the latter category. It provides a significant amount of soft benefits most of which are not immediately obvious and cannot have a monetary value attached to them.

16.3 The strategic and economic benefits of groupware

Groupware is perhaps unique in the IT world because it not only provides a wide range of business benefits but can ultimately change the shape, structure, culture and long-term future of an organisation. It can provide the short-term economic benefits (hard benefits) that are required within an organisation and are usually the basis for all investments but it has the potential to provide many long-term strategic benefits (soft benefits) as well. It is these soft benefits that are interesting organisations and making them consider a groupware solution more carefully.

The benefits of groupware can thus be categorised into soft and hard benefits with hard benefits being easily identified and soft benefits being more long term, intrinsic and hard to put a figure on. The benefits of groupware can also be categorised along an alternative or additional dimensions. Groupware can affect all aspects of an organisation from its strategic direction, through its operational procedures to the way that employees work in their daily lives. Groupware therefore affects the strategic, operational and personal levels within an organisation.

It is important to remember that is not the groupware products that will bring the advantages to an organisation, it is the way in which the organisation exploits the potential of the products.

> "There's no such thing as groupware. It's not a product, it's what you make of it" [*Dave Kearns, information services manager, Thomas Conrad Corp.*].

16.3.1 Hard benefits

Hard business benefits are those which provide short term, measurable gain, mainly in the form of cost savings or increased productivity. Groupware implementations will almost always provide cost savings because information will be made more widely available in electronic form which reduces the costs of stationery and the associated filing space required.

Strategic level benefits

- Increased revenue - the introduction of groupware promises to improve productivity, reduce costs, improve customer service and increase the competitiveness and adaptability of an organisation. In doing so, the ultimate result will be an improvement in revenue and profitability. Groupware also provides the incentive for streamlining the business to maximise efficiency and profit margins.
- Increased market share - groupware implementations are still incredibly new and the technology is still not widely understood or fully utilised. Organisations therefore have the potential to use groupware as a means of getting ahead of the competition by introducing radical changes into the organisation and making the competition ask "How on earth did they do that?". Using groupware as an enabler for revolutionary changes in work practices and culture is very high risk but can lead to a substantial increase in market share and sales - primarily due to the organisation's ability to respond immediately to customer requirements.
- Less training time - the introduction of groupware usually involves the company wide standardisation on key software products such as word processors, spreadsheets, PC databases and presentation packages. These all have common user interfaces which will continue to be emulated in emerging groupware products with consistency being of major importance. This means that once users are trained in the use of such packages, migrating to a new version or a new product with a similar interface will require the minimum amount of additional training. Once users have become familiar with the concept of working in a team, the adoption of other work group products will also require minimal re-training and will lead to a more IT educated and motivated work force.

Operational level benefits

- Reduced costs - every business continually strives to reduce their costs and keep them at the lowest possible level. This ensures that they remain competitive and reducing costs can also help to increase margins and hence profits. The introduction of IT usually results in a reduction of costs through space or labour savings and groupware is no exception. Groupware allows people to work more efficiently - the same number of people can be more productive or fewer people will be needed to maintain the same level of productivity. Keeping more information in an electronic form and making it more widely available reduces the need for storage and archiving space.

- Improved productivity - in addition to keeping costs at a minimum, businesses are also concerned with maintaining and improving productivity levels. To date, IT spend has not been rewarded with a significant improvements in productivity although the introduction of groupware promises change this trend. By allowing individuals to work as a team, by distributing business information throughout all levels of an organisation and by redesigning processes to exploit groupware, the same number of people will become more productive or produce a higher quality service.

Personal level benefits

- Increased Personal Productivity - the overall increase in productivity that is likely to arise from a groupware implementation obviously stems from a rise in personal productivity. Groupware allows employees to work in teams based around redesigned business processes with the autonomy to make their own day-to-day decisions. Teams are more productive than individuals working in isolation and the team environment increases employee morale and enthusiasm.
- Increased Autonomy - empowering teams gives users more autonomy and control over their day-to-day activities. This autonomy will allow them to redesign their work procedures and environment to suit their needs and will give them more responsibility for determining their own destiny. Users, especially those involved in knowledge work, have been demanding this form of autonomy for a long time and groupware provides the cultural and structural changes necessary for it to be given.
- Increased Flexibility - operating in a team environment means that teams can be built and disbanded as demand requires with employees able to respond positively to the changes.

16.3.2 Soft benefits

Many organisations are using groupware to restructure, reorganise and change the future path of their organisation. Groupware allows organisations to get 'out of a rut'. It facilitates the redesign of business processes and the restructuring of management hierarchies to take advantage of a network management structure and empowered teams. Some organisations are implementing groupware in the knowledge that there will be no immediate benefits but are anticipating that the long term benefits will be significant.

Strategic level benefits

- Improved customer satisfaction - groupware enables an organisation to create a corporate database - the corporate memory - which everybody has access to. Employees who deal directly with customers will have the information that they need instantly available and will have access to more information than before. This will enable them to provide a better service to the customer and respond more quickly to customer queries, concerns and requests.
- Improved public image - groupware technology is still relatively new and large scale groupware implementations are regarded as highly prestigious. A groupware implementation can therefore provide a company with a improved public image.
- More responsive organisation - establishing a team working structure around reengineered processes makes an organisation more responsive to changing market conditions. Changes can be accommodated by the establishing of teams and the immediate modification of well understood business processes.
- More adaptable organisation - the change that occurs in an organisation during the move to groupware makes it more responsive to dramatic change but also means that it is more adaptable to any fluctuations in its market place.

Operational level benefits

- Increased access to information - one of the main objectives and benefits of groupware is in introducing the information sharing culture and organisational memory. The capabilities of the organisational memory are endless and by using groupware products to interface with the outside world, the number of sources of information that can be drawn from is only limited by those that can be accessed.

- Improved communications - groupware provides communications facilities to allow employees to communicate effectively regardless of time and place. The improved communication channels means that information is passed between employees more quickly and more easily. It is also likely that there will be fewer meetings held and those that are will be shorter and more productive.
- Improved structure and culture - the introduction of groupware provides an organisation with the opportunity to restructure itself and adopt the culture of collaborative individualism. The organisation can operate with fewer levels of management and drive power down through the hierarchies until users are given the autonomy they need to successfully carry out their business function.

Personal level benefits

- Improved employee morale - the adoption of the new management structure and culture of team working will undoubtedly increase employee morale. Groupware will also provide employees with the tools that they need to work effectively in a team and will provide them with access to the information that they require. Employees operating in a groupware environment have more autonomy and responsibility for their day-to-day actions and have the freedom to adapt their working procedures to those that suit their way of working.
- Increased individual responsibility - employees may be given the responsibility for defining their own working practices, training and development programmes, aims, goals and objectives and may even be responsible for recruitment.
- Increased feeling of employee participation in decision making - by empowering teams, you give them greater control over their day-to-day lives. You also give them the opportunity to make suggestions, air their concerns and generally to play a more important role in the decision-making process.

16.3.3 Additional benefits

Other benefits that have been reported from groupware implementations are:

- systems will become more attuned to the needs of the human user
- smaller, more autonomous teams can take more initiatives
- physical location of employees will be less of a constraint on organisational structures
- enhanced team working may allow products to be developed and altered more quickly
- the improved communication links and the increased autonomy given to workers will mean that more ideas are generated and followed up
- reduced cost of labour and travel time
- better quality of decisions
- improved process control
- shorter product development cycles.

16.4 Summary

In this section we have presented the risks that are associated with a groupware project and attempted to give advice on how they can be avoided. We have described the modern techniques which can be used to justify high tech IT investments and provide a framework for assessing the benefits. We have also listed the potential benefits that groupware can bring.

A single groupware implementation will obviously not realise all of the benefits given above but groupware technology and the enabling hardware products do have the potential to reward an organisation with each and every one if implemented correctly.

Section VII. Conclusions and look to the future

Chapter 17. Groupware is here to stay

Whether you like it or not, groupware is here and it appears as though it is here to stay. As we enter the next century, businesses will increasingly demand greater input and productivity from their staff and this will require them to cooperate and join their efforts in achieving well defined and engineered business processes.

Working together cohesively is made possible by the advent of groupware which supports interactions any time, any place. This point is becoming more important as business become global with operations interacting across disparate locations and time zones. Groupware products of the future may even incorporate facilities to cope with language and even perhaps cultural differences.

The impact that groupware will have on the modern business - the business must be modern in its views if it is to adopt a widespread groupware solution - is hard to imagine but it may be so great as to make the office of the 1990s a thing of the past.

Dinosaur companies - those that think groupware is a fad and refuse to be drawn into the team working philosophy - will soon be left behind by competitors who have adopted a groupware type environment. Such companies will be more flexible, more responsive, more customer facing, and have a more productive work force and a better motivated one. They will also be in tune with their customers and suppliers who will also have turned to a groupware solution (even if this is just the mass use of electronic information rather than paper).

Groupware is a new area of IT and is therefore still not widely understood. The reports in the press, computer magazines and journals tend to focus on telling people that groupware will have an impact on their business and that they must prepare themselves for it. What they refrain from telling the reader is what exactly the impact will be, how exactly the organisation can prepare for it and what exactly the organisation can do to overcome it. They are also not in the habit of informing people how to go about successfully implementing groupware.

We hope that we have changed this situation by providing a framework, in the form of the Groupware Pyramid Principle, which can be used to progress through a groupware implementation to a successful, beneficial, measurable and flexible conclusion.

We would like to round off the book by just thinking about the office of the future and what the characteristics of it might be. There is much speculation about this point and we have made further in the content of this book. But with the office playing such an important part of everybody's lives, it is worth spending time pondering on this thought and using these thoughts to plan for your own future and perhaps those of your children.

17.1 What is the office of the future?

We have already talked extensively about the modern day office and noted its limitations. We have also spent some time discussing how it may change in the future to incorporate new technology and the implementation of groupware.

The office will change in the future, possibly along the following lines:

17.1.1 Smaller, rural offices

The introduction of small, portable computers, high speed modems, wireless communication and advanced messaging tools means that more workers will be able to work equally, if not more, effectively from their own home. This will reduce office space costs for employers and will offer many benefits to employees. Teleworking is set to grow in popularity over the next few years as more employers realise that working from home is not the easy option. This will mean that the required office space will shrink to a fraction of what is required today and that big, posh offices in the city can be replaced by small, quaint, pleasant surroundings in many rural areas. In fact, what will offices be used for: to entertain clients, to house the receptionists (will the telephone still be a medium of business communication?) or to merely use as a postal address (will hand delivered post remain a medium of business communication?).

17.1.2 Paperless? - we don't think so

Paper is still in abundance in all offices and does clog the arteries of every organisation. It costs money to produce printed output, money to file printed output, money to store printed output and money to search and retrieve printed output. It is for these reasons that many organisations are adopting the new technologies which can help them to discard many paper bound activities, replacing them with automated electronic information routing. There may be a big initial expenditure to purchase such equipment, but the savings in terms of time, space and required labour can be enormous.

We believe that the truly paperless office is a long way off yet. To achieve this would require all the customers and suppliers of a company to adopt the technology, for all the staff's culture of reading script from a page to be changed, for much more sophisticated Optical Character Recognition technology (OCR) to be developed and for business processes to be fully reengineered to operate with electronic rather than paper information flows.

Some forward thinking, high-tech organisations may achieve paperless internal procedures in the very near future but, looking at the facts, the truly paperless office is only on the very distant horizon.

17.1.3 Built around teams

Modern day offices are still very much centred around the individual. Each office worker has their own PC with their own repository of information on it, each has their own job title, function and responsibilities, each has the individual monetary incentive to do better (if there is a wider section or department incentive then they are usually not in a position to affect this in any way) and each has their own desk - their own environment. This situation is likely to change in the future as individuals in offices are required to work together in tight collaboration. This will demand a new skill set from office workers who will be forced to trust their peers, to recognise, positively, the achievements of their peers, to carry out actions for the good of a broader group than themselves, to and learn to rely on their colleagues.

Workers will not have their own environment as information and objects will be shared and made available to all. Desks may no longer be personal but may be such that anyone can operate from them. This will all be happening within new and relatively untested management techniques that give great responsibility to lower echelon workers in achieving specified business objectives.

17.1.4 Operating irrespective of location

The introduction of groupware will enable offices to operate irrespective of their location and the time zone that they are in. This will perhaps mean that we develop 24 hour offices which can service the multinational needs of large organisations at any time of day.

Whether or not these or any other speculations realise themselves in the next century, there is one thing we can be sure of: the inevitable widespread implementation of groupware products, philosophies and environments into organisations will change the way we work and the environment in which we work.

Glossary of terms

The following is a list of most of the terms used throughout this book with brief explanations.

Activity processors	These are computer programs which support the organised and structured activity of groups by means of 'activity scripts' for each participant.
Agents	Intelligent software programs which provide some form of service without the users being aware of their existence. They run in the background and usually relieve users of routine information management tasks such as routing electronic mail.
Any time, any place	In 1988, Johansen produced a model which analysed group working into four categories ranging between same time, same place and different time, different place. The software advances of recent years have allowed us to consider products which are appropriate for interaction 'any time, any place'.
Applications Programming Interface (API)	APIs define the way in which programmers can interface with a product. The use and development of APIs is a way to achieve totally Open Systems (q.v.).
Asynchronous	Asynchronous events occur at different times with no coordination.
Bandwidth	Technically, this is the frequency range which a circuit can cope with. It relates to the amount of information that can be passed across a communications medium. As bandwidth increases so does the potential to send more complex data with greater efficiently.

Best of breed Best of breed products are those applications most appropriate for the particular task. Many organisation do not want to be forced to use proprietary software and instead want the opportunity to choose the applications which best suit their business processes. This means the use of open systems.

Brainstorming A technique used as the first step in solving some problem. It involves the uninhibited generation of ideas at first (no idea is a bad idea) with these ideas then being categorised and evaluated.

Bulletin board Bulletin boards are a way to have discussions with people, via computers, regardless of time or location. By using public bulletin boards such as Compulink Information Exchange (CIX) or CompuServe, you can have discussions with a large number of people and access a vast store of shared information.

Calendar systems Effective workgroup computing requires the use of scheduling facilities. An electronic calendar is part of this and allows team members to keep track of each other's activities.

Client-server computing Client-server computing is growing in popularity. It is an advanced form of server networking where the intelligence is split between the client work station and the server back-end. Clients typically request services from the server with the server performing the processes to service that request.

Coauthoring systems The same as joint authoring, these systems support the simultaneous use of documents by two or more people.

Collaboration The way in which two or more people cooperate together on one or more specific tasks.

Collaborative computing This is another term used in place of groupware to describe systems which support users working in teams.

Computer aided teams Groups of people working together supported by methods, information and communication technology, based on insights into the human group working process.

Computer Output to Laser Disk (COLD) Optical storage media is of extremely high capacity and is no longer out of the average department's budget range. Archiving or storing information on laser or optical disks is an efficient storage method and means that the data is readily available.

Computer Supported Cooperative Working (CSCW) CSCW is similar in nature to groupware but emphasises the analysis of teams and using information technology to support these teams. Groupware evolved from research into this field which is still very active.

Conferencing A form of electronic messaging, conferencing in generic terms allows people to communicate with each other in real-time, irrelevant of location from their desktops. This can be merely the exchange of textual messages or video and image.

Decision Support Systems (DSS) These are computer based systems which aid in decision making processes.

Desktop conferencing The use of a shared screen of information, together with an integrated voice link, by two or more people to undertake one or more specific tasks.

Document Image Processing (DIP) Document image processing technology is closely related to workflow management systems and allows paper documents to be scanned into the computer system and them maintained electronically. When connected to workflow systems, these electronic documents can be automatically routed to the people who need them.

Downsizing This is currently a popular trend in business that involves moving IT operations from the mainframe to a usually more cost effective networked environment. Rightsizing is a closely related term

E-Mail Perhaps the most basic form of electronic messaging but none-the-less a very important one which must be present in a organisation to form the basis for effective team working.

Empowering teams Currently a buzz phrase used to describe the process of moving decision making down to the end-user so that they can make fast and accurate decisions and therefore provide better customer service. In order to empower end-users, they must be provided with the necessary information and the tools to access this information. Groupware can help to make this information available.

Enterprise network A network covering the whole organisation usually built by connected LANs together with WANs. In order to share information effectively across the whole organisation, an enterprise network is necessary.

Executive Information Systems (EIS) EISs are used to extract data from what may be a huge corporate database. Business executives will only want to see a subset of this data in an easily understandable way and EISs provide this facility.

File server A computer providing a file store in server networking.

Four square model The model developed by Johansen to analyse business tasks into four categories ranging from between those that occur at the same time, same place to those that occur at a different time, different place.

Group Decision Support System (GDSS) Groupware software which enables decisions to be made more easily. This generally involves providing electronic meeting facilities such as electronic voting and brainstorming tools. It has been proved that the anonymity provided by these tools makes people less shy and more creative.

Groupwork design Procedures and guidelines to support the process of analysing the workings of a group.

Groupware Describes the categories of software which proactively support individuals that wish to work in teams. Such software usually provides the means for team members to communicate, cooperate and share information effectively.

Hierarchical management This is the traditional style of management which has dominated organisations for the past thirty years or so. It involves having several layers of management between the executives and the workers. The introduction of groupware is helping in the process of making this management style slowly redundant.

Human Computer Interface (HCI) HCI is a very active field of computer research and combines techniques from many other disciplines such as psychology and sociology, to produce computer interfaces which maximise usability and aim to extend the human mind.

Information Technology (IT) IT is the term used to describe almost anything connected with the computing industry. In simple terms, it describes the use of technology in exploiting information.

IT infrastructure The IT infrastructure of an organisation is the set of computers, networking and telecommunications which are in place to provide services to users. Many organisation do not have the necessary infrastructure to proceed with a large groupware implementation.

Knowledge worker Knowledge workers are those employees involved in quite complex tasks which require a high degree of skill and knowledge. Much of this knowledge will be personal and knowledge workers will not be forthcoming in making it available to a wider audience.

Legacy system This is the current buzz word to describe the old software and hardware systems that an organisation uses. It generally refers to mainframes and the applications running on them.

Local Area Network (LAN) A local area network typically links a relatively small number of workstations or PCs within the confines of a room, a floor of a building, an office or a site. Connection outside of a site would usually be achieved by using a Wide Area Network.

Management Information Systems (MIS) These are similar to executive information systems in that they report on data. MISs usually produce static reports at given intervals rather than providing ad hoc reporting facilities

Massively Parallel Processing (MPP) The step up from SMP systems (q.v.) is to employ hundreds of CPUs and have them all processing in parallel with tasks being shared among them.

Meeting room systems The collection of IT systems which support all aspects of face-to-face meetings including electronic tools such as voting and brainstorming.

Multi-media Multi-media involves the use of video, voice, graphics and other complex data types in communications. As the available bandwidth of communications grows, so more multi-media data is being sent and received. The next generation of groupware software will provide facilities for integrated multi-media support.

Network management A new and growing style of management where the traditional management hierarchy is flattened by the removal of layers of middle management. More responsibility is given to the end users and as a result the organisation becomes more responsive. Groupware helps in the process of moving to a networked organisation because it facilitates team working and user empowerment.

Object-oriented Object-oriented technology is gaining in popularity and involves the use of objects to represent real-world entities. It also involves these objects containing the information and instructions necessary to carry out their task. This means that a user will only have to know how to use an object and can be oblivious to how it actually performs the task.

Office Automation (OA) Office automation systems aim to increase worker productivity by providing them with a standard set of sophisticated tools on their desktop. Typically applications are word processing, spreadsheet software and e-mail facilities. Groupware differs from OA in that it concentrates on the group rather than the individual.

Open Database Connectivity (ODBC)
This is a Microsoft standard which provides a uniform SQL interface to a wide range of database management systems.

Open systems
Open systems are those whose ability to communicate or interact conforms with the relevant open systems standards.

Open systems architecture
Many organisations do not want to be tied to using proprietary software and instead want the option of using best of breed applications. In order to have this option, a open systems architecture needs to be adopted with products chosen that conform to open systems standards and interface with a wide range of products.

Operating systems
The suite of software packages which manage your interaction with the underlying hardware of your computer. Popular PC operating systems are DOS, Windows, OS/2 and Unix.

Peer-to-peer networking
A network structure where workstations are not linked to a central server but are linked to each other in some way. This means that the local data on each workstation can be accessed by other workstations and local resources are available to all workstations. This is very good way of sharing resources such as printers in a small organisation.

Pilot project
A pilot project is a small project which is carried out to test the appropriateness of some new technology. A pilot project should aim to highlight the benefits of the new technology and should be implemented with enthusiastic, committed users.

Process modelling
The modelling of a business process usually using a formal methodology. This can form the first step of business process reengineering. Workflow automation software can help with this task.

Prototyping A method of developing small systems rapidly. This usually works well in the situation where the application needs to be developed quickly and with a small user population. The problem comes when the organisation tries to develop the prototype further with a bigger user population. This usually ends in disaster and requires a whole new design.

Psychology This is the science which studies human behaviour and thought processes.

Responsive organisation Allied to the network management style, a responsive organisation is one where end-users are empowered with the information and authority necessary to provide immediate service to customers. It is also an organisation built around teams where teams can be set up and disbanded as required to meet market conditions.

Rightsizing This is similar in nature to downsizing but involves placing applications on the environment on which they will operate at their most cost effective.

Scaleablity This is an important and desirable feature of both software and hardware systems. Scaleable systems can be increased in size, power and complexity with ease and without the need to invest significant amounts in additional software and hardware products.

Scanner An electronic device which will convert paper documents into a digital equivalent so that the electronic image can be passed around and the paper version does not have to be stored.

Scheduling A category of groupware software which enables people to maintain electronic diaries and calendars so that colleagues can automatically check on their availability and also automatically schedule meetings and the resources for those meetings.

Screen sharing systems Enable users, from their workstation, to access and sometimes manipulate the information being displayed on the screen of another workstation.

Server networking A network structure in which a specialised machine (server) provides services such as processing facilities and file storage to the connected workstations and PCs.

Shared information systems Provide support for total information sharing by allowing the members of a group unlimited access to shared information.

Shelfware These are products that are particularly attractive to buy but are difficult to implement. Therefore, they sit around on the shelf waiting for the right moment or person to come along and make use of them. Groupware products have been described as shelfware with applications such as Lotus Notes being purchased by organisations who then find it difficult to find an area to exploit it. This situation can be avoided by purchasing groupware software that addresses a specific business problem and not by finding a business problem once the software has been bought.

Sociology The field of research involving the study of group life and social organisation.

Symmetric Multi Processing (SMP) The new method of increasing the speed of central processing units is to link several CPUs together and to share processing tasks among them. This involves creating a symmetric multi processing environment.

Synchronous Synchronous events occur in coordination with each other, usually at specified times or the same time.

Tele-working This is the term referring to the practice of working away from the office either at home or on a mobile basis with communication being maintained by some electronic form. As the cost of office space increases, tele-working could become a popular option. The psychological aspects of isolation are important here.

Unstructured information Much of the information that we process in our daily lives is unstructured in the form of paper communications, visual images and conversations. Up until now, computer systems have concentrated only on structured information that can be stored in traditional databases. Groupware software attempts to capture unstructured information so that it can be used as part of the corporate information database.

Value Added Network (VAN) VANs provide access to host-based services provided by an independent network services supplier.

Vapourware Vapourware products are those which are announced by vendors but which never actually become available to the public until a much later date if at all. Because of the current popularity of groupware, many vendors are claiming that they will release revolutionary products without actually producing the goods. Beware of designing your groupware systems based on announcements of vapourware.

Video conferencing A form of messaging where a meeting can be carried out across remote locations with video images being provided on people's desktops to give them the effect of a face-to-face meeting. This technology can save a lot of time and money by reducing the travelling costs associated with attending meetings located elsewhere.

Virtual company A virtual company is one built on the basis of tele-working where the central office is extremely small and most of the workers operate remotely. This has been made a realistic possibility by the advances in communications and groupware technology.

Virtual teams The formation of teams of experts as and when the need arises. These teams can then be disbanded when they are no longer required. The formation of the team does not take a team member away from their desk because groupware allows teams to work together effectively even if the participants are distributed geographically

Wide Area Network (WAN) This is a network which covers a wide geographical area and usually links many LANs together. WANs have the capability of providing reliable and efficient links around the world.

Workflow The flow of documents or information around an office or organisation in a prescribed order.

Workflow automation A category of groupware technology which can take manual office workflows and automate these procedures. This involves automatically routing the documents to the appropriate places and keeping track of where they are.

Workgroup computing Another term to describe groupware which emphasises the process of organising a business around productive teams, using computer support to facilitate cooperative working and to eliminate the restrictions of time and space.

WYSIWIS (What You See Is What I See) This is an adaptation of the familiar WYSIWYG concept where everybody sharing a document simultaneously will automatically see the amendments made by one of their colleagues. Providing this service requires extremely sophisticated software to enable the interaction and to prevent update anomalies.

Bibliography

Apricot (1993)	Apricot Computers, *The Book of Workgroup Computing,* 1993
Augustine et al. (1993)	Fred K. Augustine Jr, Theodore J. Surynt, Frank A. Dezoort and Daniel K. Rosetti, "Organisational Impact of Decision Support Technology: What's Ahead for the '90s?", *Journal of End User Computing* ,Spring 1993
Bartram and Youett (1993)	Peter Bartram and Chris Youett, *The Groupware Report '93*, Policy Publications, 1993
Bate and Burgess (1985)	Joseph St John Bate and Ross Burgess, *The Automated Office*, Collins, 1985
Blake (1992)	Lanny Blake, "Reduce Employees' Resistance to Change", *Personnel Journal*, September 1992
Bray (1994)	Paul Bray, "Face Value", *Which Computer*, March 1994
Brown and Watts (1992)	James H. Brown and Julian Watts, "Enterprise Engineering: Building 21st Century Organisations", *Journal of Strategic Information Systems*, December 1992
Bryant (1993)	Jim Bryant, "Supporting Management Teams", *OR Insight,* July/September 1993
Carr (1992)	Clay Carr, "Planning Priorities for Empowered Teams", *Journal of Business Strategy*, 1992
Cass, Heintz and Kaiser (1992)	Kimberley Cass, Timothy J. Heintz and Kate M. Kaiser, "An Investigation of Satisfaction when using a Voice-Synchronous GDSS in Dispersed Meetings", *Information and Management,* 1992

Dallas (1992) Karl Dallas, "Getting IT", *Personal Computer Magazine*, June 1992

Dayton (1991) Doug Dayton, "Power to the People", *PC Week Special Report: Groupware,* October 1991

Dempsey (1993) Michael Dempsey, "The Prize Groupware Delivers", *Financial Times,* June 1993

Donelan (1993) Joseph Donelan, "Using Electronic Tools to Improve Meetings", *Management Accounting,* March 1993

DTI (1994) Department of Trade and Industry, *Computer Supported Cooperative Work Awareness Initiative,* 1994

Dyson (1990) Esther Dyson, "Why Groupware Is Gaining Ground", *Datamation*, March 1990

Ellis et al. (1991) C.A. Ellis, S.J. Gibbs and G.L. Rein, "Groupware: Some Issues and Experiences", *Communications of the ACM,* January 1991

Englebart (1988) Douglas Englebart, "Bootstrapping and the Handbook Cycle", *Proc. CSCW Conference 1988*

Gould (1993) Lawrence Gould, "Enterprise Management", *Managing Automation,* July 1993

Gould (1991) Michael Gould, "What is Groupware Anyway?", *PC Week Special Report: Groupware,* October 1991

Hammer and Champy (1993) Michael Hammer and James Champy, *Reengineering the Corporation,* N. Brealey Publishers, 1993

Hsu and Lockwood (1993) Jeffrey Hsu and Tony Lockwood, "Collaborative Computing", *Byte,* March 1993

Janson (1991) Jennifer L. Janson, "ROI: Costs vs. Benefits", *PC Week Special Report: Groupware,* October 1991

Johnsen-Lenz (1982) Peter and Trudy Johnsen-Lenz, *Consider the Groupware: Design and Group Process Impacts on Communication in the Electronic Medium*, 1982

Johnson-Lenz (1992)	Peter and Trudy Johnson-Lenz, "Groupware is Computer-Mediated Culture: Some Keys to Using it Wisely", *Proc. Conference on Groupware 1992, San Jose, California*, 1992
Jones and Kaye (1993)	Phil Jones and John Kaye, "Getting into the Group", *Infomatics*, February 1993
Kavanagh (1992)	John Kavanagh, *Financial Times,* (30 September 1992)
Liardet and Morris (1993)	Mike Liardet and Pete Morris, "Going with the Flow," *Personal Computer Magazine,* September 1993
Limerick (1991)	David Limerick, "The Shape of the New Organisation", *Proc. IPMA National Conference*, 1991
Mill (1993)	Jenny Mill, "Dual Control", *Computing,* April 1993
Montebello and Buzzotta (1993)	Anthony R. Montebello and Victor R. Buzzotta, "Work Teams that Work", Training and Development (March 1993)
Pasmore (1993)	William A. Pasmore, "Designing Work Systems for Knowledge Workers", *Journal for Quality and Participation,* July/August 1993
PC Plus (1993)	PC Plus, *PC Plus, Workgroup Computing Supplement*, November 1993
Peltu (1992)	Malcolm Peltu, "Conquering Space", *Computing*, October 1992
Perugia (1993)	Peter Perugia, "DIP Workflow and Groupware Strategy", *Information Management and Technology,* 1993, **26**, No. 5
Reinhardt (1993)	Andy Reinhardt, "Smarter E-Mail is Coming", *Byte,* 1993
Robbins (1992)	Lee Robbins, "Designing More Functional Organisations: The 12 Step Model", *Journal of Organisational Change Management* 1992, **5**, No. 4
Roberts (1993)	Mark Roberts, *Groupware: Innovative New Technology or Mutton Dressed as Lamb*, PA Consulting Group White Paper, May 1993

Sharpe (1993)	Richard Sharpe, "Groupware: Cooperative Society", *Computer Weekly,* June 1993
Shephard (1993)	Garth Shephard, "Workgroup Products and Applications", *IBM PC User Group*, 25 February 1993
Thompson and Strickland (1990)	A.A Thompson and A.J. Strickland, *Strategic Management: Concepts and Cases* (5th ed), BPI Irwin, 1990
Vincent (1993)	Geoff Vincent, "Groupware in the 21st Century", *PA Consulting Group White Paper,* January 1993
Wellins (1992)	Richard S. Wellins, "Building a Self-Directed Work Team", *Training and Development*, December 1992
Which Computer (1994)	Which Computer, "Electronic Publishing", *Which Computer,* March 1994
Whitehead (1991)	Roger Whitehead, "A Short Guide to Groupware", *Financial Times Business Information,* May 1991
Whitehead (1993)	Roger Whitehead, *Groupware News*, March/April 1993
Wilson (1991)	Paul Wilson, *Computer Supported Cooperative Work*, Intellect Books, 1991
Wright (1992)	Tim Wright, "Group Dynamics", *Which Computer*, July 1992

Index